A Note From Rick Renner

I am on a personal quest to see a "revival of the Bible" so people can establish their lives on a firm foundation that will stand strong and endure the test as end-time storm winds begin to intensify.

In order to experience a revival of the Bible in your personal life, it is important to take time each day to read, receive, and apply its truths to your life. James tells us that if we will continue in the perfect law of liberty — refusing to be forgetful hearers, but determined to be doers — we will be blessed in our ways. As you watch or listen to the programs in this series and work through this corresponding study guide, I trust you will search the Scriptures and allow the Holy Spirit to help you hear something new from God's Word that applies specifically to your life. I encourage you to be a doer of the Word He reveals to you. Whatever the cost, I assure you — it will be worth it.

> Thy words were found, and I did eat them;
> and thy word was unto me the joy and rejoicing of mine heart:
> for I am called by thy name, O Lord God of hosts.
> — Jeremiah 15:16

Your brother and friend in Jesus Christ,

Rick Renner

Unless otherwise indicated, all scripture quotations are taken from the *King James Version* of the Bible.

Scripture quotations marked (*AMPC*) are taken from the *Amplified® Bible*. Copyright © 1954, 1958, 1962, 1964, 1965, 1987 by The Lockman Foundation. Used by permission. **www.Lockman.org**.

Scripture quotations marked (ESV) are from *The Holy Bible, English Standard Version*. ESV® Text Edition: 2016. Copyright © 2001 by Crossway Bibles, a publishing ministry of Good News Publishers.

All Scripture marked with the designation (*GW*) is taken from GOD'S WORD®. © 1995, 2003, 2013, 2014, 2019, 2020 by God's Word to the Nations Mission Society. Used by permission.

Scripture quotations marked (*NIV*) are taken from *Holy Bible, New International Version*®, *NIV*® Copyright ©1973, 1978, 1984, 2011 by Biblica, Inc.® Used by permission. All rights reserved worldwide.

Scripture quotations marked (*NKJV*) are taken from the *New King James Version*®. Copyright © 1982 by Thomas Nelson. Used by permission. All rights reserved.

Scripture quotations marked (*NLT*) are taken from the Holy Bible, *New Living Translation*, copyright © 1996, 2004, 2015 by Tyndale House Foundation. Used by permission of Tyndale House Publishers, Inc., Carol Stream, Illinois 60188. All rights reserved.

10 Powerful Men

Copyright © 2021 by Rick Renner
P.O. Box 702040
Tulsa, OK 74170

Published by Rick Renner Ministries
www.renner.org

ISBN 13: 978-1-68031-906-4

eBook ISBN 13: 978-1-68031-907-1

All rights reserved. No portion of this book may be reproduced or transmitted in any form or by any means — electronic, mechanical, photocopy, recording, scanning, or other — except for brief quotations in critical reviews or articles, without the prior written permission of the Publisher.

How To Use This Study Guide

This ten-lesson study guide corresponds to *"10 Powerful Men" With Rick Renner* (Renner TV). Each lesson in this study guide covers a topic that is addressed during the program series, with questions and references supplied to draw you deeper into your own private study of the Scriptures on this subject.

To derive the most benefit from this study guide, consider the following:

First, watch or listen to the program prior to working through the corresponding lesson in this guide. (Programs can also be viewed at **renner.org** by clicking on the Media/Archives links.)

Second, take the time to look up the scriptures included in each lesson. Prayerfully consider their application to your own life.

Third, use a journal or notebook to make note of your answers to each lesson's Study Questions and Practical Application challenges.

Fourth, invest specific time in prayer and in the Word of God to consult with the Holy Spirit. Write down the scriptures or insights He reveals to you.

Finally, take action! Whatever the Lord tells you to do according to His Word, do it.

For added insights on this subject, it is recommended that you obtain *All the Men of the Bible* by Herbert Lockyer and Rick and Denise's autobiography *Unlikely: Our Faith-Filled Journey to the Ends of the Earth*. You may also select from Rick's other available resources by placing your order at **renner.org** or by calling 1-800-742-5593.

LESSON 1

TOPIC
Noah — a History Maker

SCRIPTURES
1. **2 Chronicles 16:9** — For the eyes of the Lord run to and fro throughout the whole earth, to shew himself strong in the behalf of them whose heart is perfect toward him....
2. **Genesis 6:5-8,11-14** — And God saw that the wickedness of man was great in the earth, and that every imagination of the thoughts of his heart was only evil continually. And it repented the Lord that he had made man on the earth, and it grieved him at his heart. And the Lord said, I will destroy man whom I have created from the face of the earth; both man, and beast, and the creeping thing, and the fowls of the air; for it repenteth me that I have made them. But Noah found grace in the eyes of the Lord.... The earth also was corrupt before God, and the earth was filled with violence. And God looked upon the earth, and, behold, it was corrupt; for all flesh had corrupted his way upon the earth. And God said unto Noah, The end of all flesh is come before me; for the earth is filled with violence through them; and, behold, I will destroy them with the earth. Make thee an ark of gopher wood....
3. **Hebrews 11:7** — By faith Noah, being warned of God of things not seen as yet, moved with fear, prepared an ark to the saving of his house; by the which he condemned the world, and became heir of the righteousness which is by faith.

GREEK WORDS
1. "being warned" — χρηματίζω (*chrematidzo*): a business transaction; to transact business or to advise or consult with one about important affairs; to be advised and consulted by God
2. "not seen as yet" — μηδέπω βλεπομένων (*medepo blepomenon*): not ever seen, never, ever before seen
3. "moved with fear" — εὐλαβέομαι (*eulabeomai*): to do something cautiously; to take action urgently and seriously

4. "prepared" — **κατασκευάζω** (*kataskeuadzo*): to put forth great effort to build a vessel, an ark
5. "ark" — **κιβωτός** (*kibotos*): not a ship, but a wooden box
6. "to the saving of his house" — **εἰς σωτηρίαν τοῦ οἴκου αὐτοῦ** (*eis soterian tou oikou autou*): for the explicit purpose of saving his own household

SYNOPSIS

The ten lessons in this study on *10 Powerful Men* will focus on the following individuals:

- Noah — a History Maker
- Abraham — Imperfect Father of Faith
- Samuel — a Child Called To Minister
- David — a Man With the Right Inner Makings
- Daniel — a Man Who Refused Limitations
- Joseph — the Foster Father of Jesus
- Peter — From Fisherman to Apostle
- Paul — a Murderer Turned Apostle
- Timothy — a Teen Called to Ministry
- John — the Last of the First 12 Apostles

The emphasis of this lesson:

Noah was a man who loved God and had a healthy reverential fear of Him. As a result, he found favor in God's eyes and was given prophetic insight to see what was about to happen on the earth and how to escape the coming destruction. In obedience to God, Noah prepared an ark and saved his family and a select remnant of all the land creatures.

Contrary to what many in the world believe, God *is* concerned with what goes on in people's lives. He so desperately wants to bring hope, healing, and restoration to humanity that the Bible says, "…The eyes of the Lord run to and fro throughout the whole earth, to shew himself strong in the behalf of them whose heart is perfect toward him…" (2 Chronicles 16:9).

Throughout history, there have been many individuals who have dedicated their lives to the Lord, and as a result, He has done amazing things through them. One of those individuals was a man named Noah, and his story is found in both the Old and New Testaments.

In Noah's Day, the Earth Was Utterly Corrupt

The book of Genesis gives us a picture of the condition of the earth and society during Noah's day. Thousands of years have elapsed since the dawn of creation, and the Bible says:

> **And God saw that the wickedness of man was great in the earth, and that every imagination of the thoughts of his heart was only evil continually. And it repented the Lord that he had made man on the earth, and it grieved him at his heart.**
>
> **And the Lord said, I will destroy man whom I have created from the face of the earth; both man, and beast, and the creeping thing, and the fowls of the air; for it repenteth me that I have made them.**
>
> **But Noah found grace in the eyes of the Lord.**
>
> **— Genesis 6:5-8**

Aren't you grateful for the amazing grace of God! It places us in a separate category from the rest of the world and enables us to receive His indescribable favor in our lives.

The Bible goes on to say:

> **The earth also was corrupt before God, and the earth was filled with violence. And God looked upon the earth, and, behold, it was corrupt; for all flesh had corrupted his way upon the earth.**
>
> **And God said unto Noah, The end of all flesh is come before me; for the earth is filled with violence through them; and, behold, I will destroy them with the earth.**
>
> **Make thee an ark of gopher wood....**
>
> **— Genesis 6:11-14**

Here we see God revealing to Noah in advance what He is about to do on the earth. This confirms His word through the prophet Amos, which says,

"Certainly, the Almighty Lord doesn't do anything unless he first reveals his secret to his servants…" (Amos 3:7 *GW*).

Noah Was 'Warned of God' of 'Things Not Seen'

In Hebrews 11:7, the Bible says, "By faith Noah, being warned of God of things not seen as yet, moved with fear, prepared an ark to the saving of his house; by the which he condemned the world, and became heir of the righteousness which is by faith."

In Greek, the words "being warned" are a translation of the word *chrematidzo*, which is a very unique word that describes *a business transaction*. It means *to transact business* or *to advise or consult with one about important affairs*. In this case, it means *to be advised and consulted by God*. The use of the word *chrematidzo* tells us that Noah had a businesslike relationship with God in which God was the senior partner, and Noah did what he was told. Thus, Noah literally was *being divinely advised and warned* by God "of things not seen as yet."

The phrase "not seen as yet" is a translation of the Greek words *medepo blepomenon*, which means *not ever seen*, or *never, ever before seen*. This makes total sense when we realize what God advised and warned Noah about — a worldwide flood. No one had ever seen a flood of this magnitude. In fact, they hadn't even seen rain! Prior to the flood, the vegetation was watered by a mist that came up from the ground (*see* Genesis 2:5,6). Thus, the concept of a catastrophic deluge sounded extremely bizarre to Noah and all those who heard about it.

To get ready for what was coming, God instructed Noah to build an ark, which was also something he and everyone else had never seen or heard of. Moreover, God told Noah to collect two of every kind of animal — a male and a female — and bring them into the ark. He was also to gather food for the animals and for his family. All these unprecedented tasks were assigned to Noah and his family members, and they required a tremendous amount of resources, time, and labor to execute.

Noah Stayed in His Place of Faith

To accomplish this God-sized assignment, Noah needed to stay in his place of faith for a very long time. It seems the ark's construction took at least a hundred years, and more than likely, Noah used his resources to employ a sizable work force to get the job done. Can you imagine the money, the manpower, and the time it would take to gather all that was needed to build the ark?

Throughout the process, there were probably times when Mrs. Noah said, "Noah, are you absolutely sure God has spoken to you and asked you to do this?" Possibly even his sons said, "Uh, Dad… We're giving our lives for all this, and we've become the laughingstock of the community. Do you know without question that God spoke to you?"

It is almost certain that people laughed at Noah and his sons. Remember, Scripture says Noah was "a preacher of righteousness" (2 Peter 2:5). He was a prophet who prophesied that a worldwide flood was going to come and destroy the earth and everything in it. No one had ever even heard of such a thing — neither had they ever seen an ark being built or the parade of animals that gathered in Noah's community. These things must have seemed extremely bizarre to all the bystanders.

The truth is there were forces all around Noah, pulling on him and trying to get him to let go of and back away from what God had spoken to him. This was especially true of the people in the world around him. Yet regardless of the world's criticism, the questions from his family, and even the personal concerns that weighed on his mind, Noah rejected it all and chose to trust what God, his senior partner, had said. His faith pleased God and landed him a place in God's Hall of Faith found in Hebrews 11.

Moved With Fear, Noah Prepared an Ark

What else does Hebrews 11:7 say about Noah? It says, "…Moved with fear, [he] prepared an ark to the saving of his house; by the which he condemned the world, and became heir of the righteousness which is by faith." The phrase "moved with fear" is a translation of the Greek word *eulabeomai*, and it means *to do something cautiously; to take action urgently and seriously*. Noah knew that he had heard from God, and he was quick to obey. He was not afraid for himself; he simply had a sense of awe and responsibility to do as he had been instructed.

Also notice the word "prepared." It is the Greek word *kataskeuadzo*, which means *to put forth great effort*. In this case, it means *Noah put forth great effort to build a vessel, an ark*. Thus, Noah gave everything he had in order to construct the ark, building it exactly according to the plan God had given him. The word "ark" in Greek is *kibotos*. It is not the word for a ship, but *a wooden box*. The ark was *an enormous wooden container* — not for sailing, but for warehousing and saving what it contained. And this container included Noah and his family, multitudes of animals, food for the trip, and a sewage system of some kind.

Hebrews 11:7 says that by faith, Noah built the ark "to the saving of his house." That literally means *for the explicit purpose of saving his own household*. Out of the entire population of the earth at that time, only eight people survived the Great Flood: Noah, his wife, his three sons and their wives. Noah and his family were the only ones *not affected* by God's judgment on the world. They were the righteous remnant.

Eventually the day came when God spoke to Noah and told him to take his family and go into the ark. The Bible says, "…and the Lord shut him in" (Genesis 7:16). Once Noah did his part, God did what only God could do — He sealed the door. Suddenly, the rain began to fall and fountains deep within the earth began to burst forth and flood the world. It wasn't long before the waters collected around the ark and lifted it off the ground. Noah and his family and all the animals that were with them literally floated on the waters of destruction.

For about one year, Noah and his family were kept safe within the ark. When the flood waters finally receded, God told him, "Go out of the ark, you and your wife, and your sons and your sons' wives with you" (Genesis 8:16 *NKJV*). One can only imagine the muddy mess they encountered as they emerged from the ark. Clearly, the world looked nothing like it had before the flood. It had been under water for nearly a year, causing the landscape of the earth to be significantly changed.

Just as it took faith to build the ark and preserve a remnant of all the animal kinds, it also took faith for Noah and his family to repopulate the earth. Was Noah perfect? No. But his heart was bent in the direction of obeying the Lord, and the Lord showed Himself strong on his behalf.

In our next lesson, we will focus on the life of Abraham — imperfect father of faith.

STUDY QUESTIONS

> Study to shew thyself approved unto God, a workman that needeth not to be ashamed, rightly dividing the word of truth.
> — 2 Timothy 2:15

1. Take time to read Genesis 6:1-12 and identify the conditions of world and the people during Noah's day. What was God's reaction to the state of society? What did Jesus say about Noah's day in Matthew 24:37-39? According to Second Peter 3:7-12, how will God bring final judgment on the world for its rejection of Him?
2. Jesus said, "…As it was in the days of Noah, so shall it be also in the days of the Son of man" (Luke 17:26). In what ways would you say the world today is like it was in Noah's day? Take some time to pause and asked God to share with you any specific instructions you need to know to prepare for the unprecedented times in which you live.

PRACTICAL APPLICATION

> But be ye doers of the word, and not hearers only, deceiving your own selves.
> —James 1:22

1. Like Noah, has God ever told you about something that was coming that you had never seen or experienced in your life? What was it? How did He instruct you to prepare for it?
2. Noah's assignment was to build an ark in order to save him and his family and a sampling of all the animals. What is *your* assignment for the *present season* you're in? Are you obediently doing it? If not, why?
3. When God called Noah to build the ark, Noah trusted Him and stayed in his place of faith for a hundred years. How long have you been trusting God and waiting for Him to come through for you? How does Noah's example inspire you to keep doing what God called you to do?
4. What if Noah had *not* obeyed God? What if he would have allowed his own uncertainty, the questioning of family, and the criticism of the world to take him out of his assignment? What might happen if you abandon what God has told you to do? Who do you think would be impacted?

LESSON 2

TOPIC
Abraham — Imperfect Father of Faith

SCRIPTURES

1. **2 Chronicles 16:9** — For the eyes of the Lord run to and fro throughout the whole earth, to shew himself strong in the behalf of them whose heart is perfect toward him….
2. **Hebrews 11:8-10** — By faith Abraham, when he was called to go out into a place which he should after receive for an inheritance, obeyed; and he went out, not knowing whither he went. By faith he sojourned in the land of promise, as in a strange country, dwelling in tabernacles with Isaac and Jacob, the heirs with him of the same promise: For he looked for a city which hath foundations, whose builder and maker is God.
3. **Genesis 12:1-4** — Now the Lord had said unto Abram, Get thee out of thy country, and from thy kindred, and from thy father's house, unto a land that I will shew thee: And I will make of thee a great nation, and I will bless thee, and make thy name great; and thou shalt be a blessing: And I will bless them that bless thee, and curse him that curseth thee: and in thee shall all families of the earth be blessed. So Abram departed, as the Lord had spoken unto him….
4. **Acts 7:2,3** — And he said, Men, brethren, and fathers, hearken; The God of glory appeared unto our father Abraham, when he was in Mesopotamia, before he dwelt in Charran, and said unto him, Get thee out of thy country, and from thy kindred, and come into the land which I shall shew thee.
5. **Galatians 3:8** — And the scripture, foreseeing that God would justify the heathen through faith, preached before the gospel unto Abraham, saying, In thee shall all nations be blessed.

GREEK WORDS

1. "called" — **καλούμενος** (*kaloumenos*): being called; to call, to invite, or to summon; depicts a summoning that requires the hearer to respond
2. "place" — **τόπος** (*topos*): a real geographical location

3. "receive" — λαμβάνω (*lambano*): to receive into one's possession; to take into one's own control and ownership; taking hold of something, grasping onto something, and embracing it so tightly that it becomes your very own
4. "obeyed" — ὑπακούω (*hupakouo*): compound of *hupo* and *akouo*; the word *hupo* means to be under and the word *akouo* means I hear; when compounded, pictures one in a subservient position who hears and obeys what is being said to him by a superior; the idea of being under authority, listening, and carrying out instructions
5. "not knowing" — μὴ ἐπιστάμενος (*me epistamenos*): the word *me* means not, and the word *epistamenos* depicts one who is on top of his subject; one who possesses professional knowledge; or one who is highly skilled and knowledgeable; in this case, one who is unacquainted, unknowledgeable, unskilled, and unprofessional in where he is going and in what he is doing
6. "sojourned" — παροικέω (*paroikeo*): to live outside the house; figuratively, to live on the street
7. "strange country" — ἀλλότριος (*allotrios*): alien; foreign; strange; unfamiliar; unnatural and even a bit weird
8. "dwelling" — κατοικέω (*katoikeo*): settling down into a home or becoming a permanent resident.
9. "tabernacles" — σκηνή (*skene*): tents

SYNOPSIS

One thing is clear: no one is perfect. The Bible says, "For all have sinned, and come short of the glory of God" (Romans 3:23). Yet, there are individuals who love God and whose hearts are open to His will and His ways. These are the people for which God is looking. Scripture says, "For the eyes of the Lord run to and fro throughout the whole earth, to shew himself strong in the behalf of them whose heart is perfect toward him…" (2 Chronicles 16:9).

In our first lesson, we saw that Noah was one person God set His eyes on and used mightily to preserve the human race and all the land creatures of the world. The next most powerful man who appears in the Bible is a man named Abraham, who was initially called Abram. Although he was a man who made many mistakes, his heart was open to God and pliable in

His hands. Like Noah, Abraham's story appears in both the Old and New Testaments.

The emphasis of this lesson:

God called Abraham to leave his country, his family, and his father's house and go to the place God would show him. Although he made many mistakes along the way, his heart was bent in obedience toward God. As a result, the Lord showed Himself strong on Abraham's behalf, making him the Father of Faith and allowing him to be the first to hear the Gospel.

God Called Abraham Out of Ur

When God first introduced Himself to Abraham, he and his wife Sarah were living in the land of Ur of the Chaldees, which was a very sophisticated and luxurious city. He was a very wealthy man, and his father, Terah, and his nephew, Lot, lived with him. The Bible says, "By faith Abraham, when he was called to go out into a place which he should after receive for an inheritance, obeyed; and he went out, not knowing whither he went" (Hebrews 11:8).

In this verse, the word "called" is the Greek word *kaloumenos*, which literally means, *being called*. It indicates *to call, to invite, or to summon*. It depicts *a summoning that requires the hearer to respond*. This tells us that Abraham could have rejected God's call and walked away. Instead, he accepted the call and with it received a supernatural revelation or enlightenment that his life had a specific purpose.

Scripture then adds that Abraham was called "…to go out into a place…" (Hebrews 11:8). The word "place" here is the Greek word *topos*, and it describes *a real geographical location*. It is from where we get the word *topographical*, as in a *topographical* map. When Abraham heard God speaking to him, he knew he needed to get into the right "place" — the right *geographic location* — in order to "receive" his inheritance.

The word "receive" in Hebrews 11:8 is a translation of the Greek word *lambano*, which means *to receive into one's possession; to take into one's own control and ownership*. It carries the idea of *taking hold of something, grasping onto something, and embracing it so tightly that it becomes your very own*. God was ready to give Abraham something, but for him to receive it, he had to reach out in faith and take ownership of it. Likewise, when

God calls you to a new assignment, you must reach out in faith and make it your own.

By Faith, Abraham Obeyed God

Hebrews 11:8 goes on to say, "…[Abraham] obeyed; and he went out, not knowing whither he went." In Greek, the word "obeyed" is *hupakouo*. It is a compound of the word *hupo*, which means *to be under*, and the word *akouo*, which means *I hear*, and is where we get the word *acoustics*. When these two words are compounded, it pictures *one in a subservient position who hears and obeys what is being said to him by a superior*. It carries the idea of *being under authority, listening, and carrying out instructions*.

Interestingly, Jesus said *six* times in the gospels and *seven* times in the book of Revelation, "He who has an ear, let him hear what the Spirit says." He is speaking to believers in the Church, which means that not all believers have ears to hear what the Holy Spirit is saying. In order to be a true Christian, Jesus is *to be Lord* of our lives, which means He is our *Supreme Master*, and we are to keep our spiritual ears open so that we can hear and obey His voice.

The use of the word *hupakouo* — translated in this verse as "obeyed" — lets us know that when God spoke to Abraham, Abraham made a decision to *listen* to God and then *to come under and submit* to God's authority, carefully carrying out His instructions. The same response is required of you. If you're going to discover and fulfill God's assignment for your life, you first need to open your ears. Once you hear God's directions, you will need to submit to His authority and carry out what He says. That is what it means to *obey*.

According to Scripture, God Told Abraham to Do Four Things

What's remarkable about Abraham's call is that there are details of what God spoke to him recorded in both the Old and New Testaments. Immediately following the account of the Tower of Babel and the disbursement of the nations, we find the overview of God's assignment to Abraham. The Bible says:

> Now the Lord had said unto Abram, Get thee out of thy country, and from thy kindred, and from thy father's house, unto a land that I will shew thee.
> — **Genesis 12:1**

This verse outlines four specific things God asked Abraham to do: (1) leave his country; (2) leave his family; (3) leave his father's home; and (4) go to the land God would show him. If Abraham would obey — if he would *submit* and come under God's authority, *listening* to and carrying out His instructions — God said He would bless Abraham in the following ways:

> And I will make of thee a great nation, and I will bless thee, and make thy name great; and thou shalt be a blessing: And I will bless them that bless thee, and curse him that curseth thee: and in thee shall all families of the earth be blessed. So Abram departed, as the Lord had spoken unto him….
> — **Genesis 12:2-4**

Unfortunately, Abraham was only partially obedient. Although he did leave his country and began heading toward the land God would show him, he didn't leave his father nor did he part ways with all of his family. Could it be that he thought to himself, *Surely God wouldn't want me to abandon my father in his old age. And Lot has been like a son to me since my brother died. I can't just leave these two family members all alone to fend for themselves. I think God would want me to take them with me.* So Abraham took his father, Terah, and his nephew, Lot, with him and delayed the fulfillment of God's plan for his life.

The Book of Acts Gives Us Extra Details About Abraham's Call

When we turn to the New Testament, we find the Holy Spirit speaking through a man by the name of Stephen, who was one of the first deacons in the Early Church. In his powerful address to the High Priest and the Jewish Council, Stephen verbally retraced Israel's history, starting with the details of Abraham's divine call. **Acts 7:2 and 3** says:

> And he said, Men, brethren, and fathers, hearken; The God of glory appeared unto our father Abraham, when he was in Mesopotamia, before he dwelt in Charran, and said unto him,

Get thee out of thy country, and from thy kindred, and come into the land which I shall shew thee.

Isn't that interesting? The glory of God appeared to Abraham *before* he lived in Harran. When he was a pagan, worshiping the moon god and living in the land of Ur of the Chaldeans (*see* Genesis 11:31), the Bible says God suddenly "appeared" to him. This word "appeared" is the Greek word *phaneros*, and it describes *something that suddenly manifests*. On that particular day, God somehow, someway suddenly showed Himself to Abraham in a misty cloud of His glory.

As Abraham was enshrouded in that glorious cloud, God not only gave him the assignment for his life, He also announced to Abraham the message of the Gospel. Galatians 3:8 says, "And the scripture, foreseeing that God would justify the heathen through faith, preached before the gospel unto Abraham, saying, In thee shall all nations be blessed." This verse tells us Abraham was the first man in all of history to hear the Gospel. He opened his ears and received the Good News from God Himself.

Abraham Didn't Know Where He Was Going

Looking once more at Hebrews 11:8, it says, "By faith Abraham, when he was called to go out into a place which he should after receive for an inheritance, obeyed; and he went out, not knowing whither he went." It's important to point out that Abraham obeyed and went out, "not knowing" where he was going.

In Greek, the phrase "not knowing" is *me epistamenos*. The word *me* means *not*, and the word *epistamenos* depicts *one who is on top of his subject; one who possesses professional knowledge*; or *one who is highly skilled and knowledgeable*. In this case, because the word *me* — meaning *not* — is in front of *epistamenos*, the original meaning is negated or reversed. Thus, the words "not knowing" describe *one who is unacquainted, unknowledgeable, unskilled, and unprofessional in where he is going and in what he is doing*. Therefore, in context of Hebrews 11:8, Abraham was *unacquainted, unknowledgeable, unskilled, and unprofessional in* "whither he went," which specifically means *where he was going* or *where he was headed*.

Hebrews 11:9 goes on to say, "By faith he sojourned in the land of promise, as in a strange country, dwelling in tabernacles with Isaac and

Jacob, the heirs with him of the same promise." The word "sojourned" is a translation of the Greek word *paroikeo*, which means *to live outside the house*. Figuratively, it means *to live on the street*. A careful study of Abraham's life reveals that he and Sarah were living on the move all the time.

The Bible says he was in a "strange country," which in Greek describes a place that is *alien; foreign, strange; unfamiliar, unnatural and even a bit weird*. You might say Abraham was like a nomad or a vagabond, "dwelling in tabernacles." The word "dwelling" is the Greek word *katoikeo*, which means *settling down into a home* or *becoming a permanent resident*. And the word "tabernacles" is the Greek term *skene*, which is the exact word for *tents*. Taking these meanings together, it seems that Abraham settled down into a pattern of living in tents.

The reason this is significant is because when God first called Abraham, he was a wealthy man who was living in the lap of luxury. Genesis 25:7 tells us that he lived 175 years. That means for the first 75 years, he lived in the opulent city of Ur. But for the remaining 100 years of his life, he lived in tents like a vagabond, wandering around looking for *the place* — the specific geographic location — God was leading him to.

It is certainly possible that as he wandered around waiting to inherit the Promised Land, he had thoughts about returning to his luxurious life in Mesopotamia. Perhaps his wife Sarah asked him a time or two, "Are you sure you heard from God? Back in Ur, we were living at ease, and now we're drifters with no place to call home. Do you really think God wants us to keep doing this?"

Yet in spite of great famines, harsh desert conditions, and wars with enemies, Abraham knew that he had heard from God and he refused to walk away from the great reward God had promised him. He never gave into the temptation to draw back from his calling. Instead, the Bible says, "He looked for a city which hath foundations, whose builder and maker is God" (Hebrews 11:10).

Yes, Abraham made many mistakes, but his heart was open to God and pliable in His hands. He learned to stay where God wanted him to be, and as a result, God showed Himself strong on Abraham's behalf, making him the Father of Faith. Friend, if you keep your heart right toward God, He will show Himself strong on your behalf too!

In our next lesson, we will look at the life of another powerful man in Scripture — the man called Samuel, who was a child God called into ministry.

STUDY QUESTIONS

> Study to shew thyself approved unto God, a workman that needeth not to be ashamed, rightly dividing the word of truth.
> — 2 Timothy 2:15

1. Abraham is actually mentioned in 27 books of the Bible. Of all the previous messages you've heard and studies you've done on his life, what do you know and appreciate most about him? What new facts about his calling and his interaction with God did you learn from this lesson?
2. What quality about Abraham do you see repeatedly mentioned in Genesis 15:6; Romans 4:3; and Galatians 3:6? Take a moment to pray and ask the Holy Spirit to help you cultivate this same quality in you.
3. History tells us that before surrendering his life to God, Abraham lived in Ur and worshiped the pagan god of the moon. What was *your* background before coming to Christ? How has He changed you since you made Him Lord of your life?

PRACTICAL APPLICATION

> But be ye doers of the word, and not hearers only, deceiving your own selves.
> — James 1:22

1. When Abraham heard God speak to him in Ur, he knew he needed to get into the right "place" — the right *geographic location* — in order to receive his inheritance. How about you? Are you in the right place to receive what God has promised? If you're not sure, pause and pray, asking Him where He wants you to be.
2. Like Abraham, do you want to know God's assignment for your life? If so, spend time in His presence and learn to "Be still, and know that [He] is God…" (Psalm 46:10). Listen carefully to what His Holy Spirit is speaking and revealing to you about your life. If God has spoken to you in the past about your assignment, ask Him to confirm it and clarify anything you may be struggling to understand.

3. Once you hear God's instructions, you need to submit to His authority and carry out what He says. Is there anything God has told you to do that you have left undone? Like Abraham, have you been *partially* obedient? If so, ask Him to forgive you and give you the grace to obediently carry out all He has said.

LESSON 3

TOPIC
Samuel — a Child Called To Minister

SCRIPTURES
1. **2 Chronicles 16:9** — For the eyes of the Lord run to and fro throughout the whole earth, to shew himself strong in the behalf of them whose heart is perfect toward him....
2. **1 Samuel 1:2-5,8-28** — And he [Elkanah] had two wives; the name of the one was Hannah, and the name of the other Peninnah: and Peninnah had children, but Hannah had no children. And this man went up out of his city yearly to worship and to sacrifice unto the Lord of hosts in Shiloh.... And when the time was that Elkanah offered, he gave to Peninnah his wife, and to all her sons and her daughters, portions: But unto Hannah he gave a worthy portion; for he loved Hannah: but the Lord had shut up her womb.... Then said Elkanah her husband to her, Hannah, why weepest thou? and why eatest thou not? and why is thy heart grieved? am not I better to thee than ten sons? So Hannah rose up after they had eaten in Shiloh, and after they had drunk. Now Eli the priest sat upon a seat by a post of the temple of the Lord. And she was in bitterness of soul, and prayed unto the Lord, and wept sore. And she vowed a vow, and said, O Lord of hosts, if thou wilt indeed look on the affliction of thine handmaid, and remember me, and not forget thine handmaid, but wilt give unto thine handmaid a man child, then I will give him unto the Lord all the days of his life, and there shall no razor come upon his head. And it came to pass, as she continued praying before the Lord, that Eli marked her mouth. Now Hannah, she spake in her heart; only her lips moved, but her voice was not heard: therefore Eli thought she had been drunken. And Eli said unto her, How long wilt thou be

drunken? put away thy wine from thee. And Hannah answered and said, No, my lord, I am a woman of a sorrowful spirit: I have drunk neither wine nor strong drink, but have poured out my soul before the Lord. Count not thine handmaid for a daughter of Belial: for out of the abundance of my complaint and grief have I spoken hitherto. Then Eli answered and said, Go in peace: and the God of Israel grant thee thy petition that thou hast asked of him. And she said, Let thine handmaid find grace in thy sight. So the woman went her way, and did eat, and her countenance was no more sad. And they rose up in the morning early, and worshipped before the Lord, and returned, and came to their house to Ramah: and Elkanah knew Hannah his wife; and the Lord remembered her. Wherefore it came to pass, when the time was come about after Hannah had conceived, that she bare a son, and called his name Samuel, saying, Because I have asked him of the Lord. And the man Elkanah, and all his house, went up to offer unto the Lord the yearly sacrifice, and his vow. But Hannah went not up; for she said unto her husband, I will not go up until the child be weaned, and then I will bring him, that he may appear before the Lord, and there abide for ever. And Elkanah her husband said unto her, Do what seemeth thee good; tarry until thou have weaned him; only the Lord establish his word. So the woman abode, and gave her son suck until she weaned him. And when she had weaned him, she took him up with her, with three bullocks, and one ephah of flour, and a bottle of wine, and brought him unto the house of the Lord in Shiloh: and the child was young. And they slew a bullock, and brought the child to Eli. And she said, Oh my lord, as thy soul liveth, my lord, I am the woman that stood by thee here, praying unto the Lord. For this child I prayed; and the Lord hath given me my petition which I asked of him: Therefore also I have lent him to the Lord; as long as he liveth he shall be lent to the Lord. And he worshipped the Lord there.

3. **1 Samuel 2:11-18,22-25** — And Elkanah went to Ramah to his house. And the child did minister unto the Lord before Eli the priest. Now the sons of Eli were sons of Belial; they knew not the Lord. And the priests' custom with the people was, that, when any man offered sacrifice, the priest's servant came, while the flesh was in seething, with a fleshhook of three teeth in his hand; And he struck it into the pan, or kettle, or caldron, or pot; all that the fleshhook brought up the priest took for himself. So they did in Shiloh unto all the Israelites that came thither. Also before they burnt the fat, the priest's servant

came, and said to the man that sacrificed, Give flesh to roast for the priest; for he will not have sodden flesh of thee, but raw. And if any man said unto him, Let them not fail to burn the fat presently, and then take as much as thy soul desireth; then he would answer him, Nay; but thou shalt give it me now: and if not, I will take it by force. Wherefore the sin of the young men was very great before the Lord: for men abhorred the offering of the Lord. But Samuel ministered before the Lord, being a child, girded with a linen ephod…. Now Eli was very old, and heard all that his sons did unto all Israel; and how they lay with the women that assembled at the door of the tabernacle of the congregation. And he said unto them, Why do ye such things? for I hear of your evil dealings by all this people. Nay, my sons; for it is no good report that I hear: ye make the Lord's people to transgress. If one man sin against another, the judge shall judge him: but if a man sin against the Lord, who shall intreat for him? Notwithstanding they hearkened not unto the voice of their father, because the Lord would slay them.

4. **1 Samuel 3:1-21** —And the child Samuel ministered unto the Lord before Eli. And the word of the Lord was precious in those days; there was no open vision. And it came to pass at that time, when Eli was laid down in his place, and his eyes began to wax dim, that he could not see; And ere the lamp of God went out in the temple of the Lord, where the ark of God was, and Samuel was laid down to sleep; That the Lord called Samuel: and he answered, Here am I. And he ran unto Eli, and said, Here am I; for thou calledst me. And he said, I called not; lie down again. And he went and lay down. And the Lord called yet again, Samuel. And Samuel arose and went to Eli, and said, Here am I; for thou didst call me. And he answered, I called not, my son; lie down again. Now Samuel did not yet know the Lord, neither was the word of the Lord yet revealed unto him. And the Lord called Samuel again the third time. And he arose and went to Eli, and said, Here am I; for thou didst call me. And Eli perceived that the Lord had called the child. Therefore Eli said unto Samuel, Go, lie down: and it shall be, if he call thee, that thou shalt say, Speak, Lord; for thy servant heareth. So Samuel went and lay down in his place. And the Lord came, and stood, and called as at other times, Samuel, Samuel. Then Samuel answered, Speak; for thy servant heareth. And the Lord said to Samuel, Behold, I will do a thing in Israel, at which both the ears of every one that heareth it shall tingle. In that day I will perform

against Eli all things which I have spoken concerning his house: when I begin, I will also make an end. For I have told him that I will judge his house for ever for the iniquity which he knoweth; because his sons made themselves vile, and he restrained them not. And therefore I have sworn unto the house of Eli, that the iniquity of Eli's house shall not be purged with sacrifice nor offering for ever. And Samuel lay until the morning, and opened the doors of the house of the Lord. And Samuel feared to shew Eli the vision. Then Eli called Samuel, and said, Samuel, my son. And he answered, Here am I. And he said, What is the thing that the Lord hath said unto thee? I pray thee hide it not from me: God do so to thee, and more also, if thou hide any thing from me of all the things that he said unto thee. And Samuel told him every whit, and hid nothing from him. And he said, It is the Lord: let him do what seemeth him good. And Samuel grew, and the Lord was with him, and did let none of his words fall to the ground. And all Israel from Dan even to Beersheba knew that Samuel was established to be a prophet of the Lord. And the Lord appeared again in Shiloh: for the Lord revealed himself to Samuel in Shiloh by the word of the Lord.

5. **1 Samuel 4:1,10-22** — ...Now Israel went out against the Philistines to battle.... And the Philistines fought, and Israel was smitten, and they fled every man into his tent: and there was a very great slaughter; for there fell of Israel thirty thousand footmen. And the ark of God was taken; and the two sons of Eli, Hophni and Phinehas, were slain. And there ran a man of Benjamin out of the army, and came to Shiloh the same day with his clothes rent, and with earth upon his head. And when he came, lo, Eli sat upon a seat by the wayside watching: for his heart trembled for the ark of God. And when the man came into the city, and told it, all the city cried out. And when Eli heard the noise of the crying, he said, What meaneth the noise of this tumult? And the man came in hastily, and told Eli. Now Eli was ninety and eight years old; and his eyes were dim, that he could not see. And the man said unto Eli, I am he that came out of the army, and I fled to day out of the army. And he said, What is there done, my son? And the messenger answered and said, Israel is fled before the Philistines, and there hath been also a great slaughter among the people, and thy two sons also, Hophni and Phinehas, are dead, and the ark of God is taken. And it came to pass, when he made mention of the ark of God, that he fell from off the seat backward by the side of the gate, and his

neck brake, and he died: for he was an old man, and heavy. And he had judged Israel forty years. And his daughter in law, Phinehas' wife, was with child, near to be delivered: and when she heard the tidings that the ark of God was taken, and that her father in law and her husband were dead, she bowed herself and travailed; for her pains came upon her. And about the time of her death the women that stood by her said unto her, Fear not; for thou hast born a son. But she answered not, neither did she regard it. And she named the child Ichabod, saying, The glory is departed from Israel: because the ark of God was taken, and because of her father in law and her husband. And she said, The glory is departed from Israel: for the ark of God is taken.

6. **1 Samuel 7:3** — And Samuel spake unto all the house of Israel….
7. **1 Samuel 7:15** — And Samuel judged Israel all the days of his life.
8. **1 Samuel 25:1** — And Samuel died; and all the Israelites were gathered together, and lamented him, and buried him in his house at Ramah….

GREEK WORDS
There are no Greek words in this lesson.

SYNOPSIS
There are no limitations on who God can and will use to see His Kingdom come and His will be done on earth as it is in Heaven. One's ethnicity, gender, or age is of no consequence. It is the *heart* of a person that is most important in God's eyes. Second Chronicles 16:9 says, "For the eyes of the Lord run to and fro throughout the whole earth, to shew himself strong in the behalf of them whose heart is perfect toward him…."

There was a time in Israel's history when God looked for a man to lead His people back into close relationship with Him, but when He couldn't find one, He chose a child. That child's name was Samuel. And from the time of his conception to his departure through death, he faithfully served the Lord in all he did, "…And the Lord was with him, and did let none of his words fall to the ground" (1 Samuel 3:19).

The emphasis of this lesson:

If there was ever a child that was longed for, it was Samuel. He was conceived in his mother's womb as a long-awaited answer to prayer and birthed at a time in Israel's history when godly leadership was desperately needed. Samuel served God's people as a prophet, a judge and a priest for many years.

Hannah Was Childless for Many Years

To understand God's selection of Samuel, we have to begin with the story of Hannah, Samuel's mother. Hannah was married to a man named Elkanah, and she deeply desired a child but was unable to become pregnant. After being barren for many years, she cried out to God in great desperation and anguish of spirit, asking Him to give her a son. The story begins in First Samuel 1:2-5:

> And he [Elkanah] had two wives; the name of the one was Hannah, and the name of the other Peninnah: and Peninnah had children, but Hannah had no children. And this man went up out of his city yearly to worship and to sacrifice unto the Lord of hosts in Shiloh…. And when the time was that Elkanah offered, he gave to Peninnah his wife, and to all her sons and her daughters, portions: But unto Hannah he gave a worthy portion; for he loved Hannah: but the Lord had shut up her womb.

Before Jerusalem became the capital of Israel, Shiloh was the center of spiritual activity. It was where the tabernacle and the Ark of the Lord were and where the high priest and judge of Israel lived and served the people. Elkanah gave each of his wives and children something significant to offer to God as a sacrifice. But when he saw that Hannah was deeply upset, he said to her, "…Hannah, why weepest thou? and why eatest thou not? and why is thy heart grieved? am not I better to thee than ten sons?" (1 Samuel 1:8).

No one knows the pain of an empty womb like a childless woman. As much as Elkanah loved Hannah, he could not grasp the severity of the sorrow she was experiencing, not to mention the tormenting aggravation she received from Peninnah, his other wife. It seems Peninnah's annoyance is what pushed Hannah to the brink of total surrender and positioned her to pray and receive the long-awaited gift of a son.

In Bitterness of Soul, Hannah Cried Out to God

Once Elkanah and Peninnah and everyone had finished their meal, the Bible says, "…Hannah rose up after they had eaten in Shiloh, and after they had drunk. Now Eli the priest sat upon a seat by a post of the temple of the Lord" (1 Samuel 1:9).

In this passage, we see that Eli was serving as high priest in Shiloh, and the Bible tells us that at this point he was old, fat, and nearly blind (*see* 1 Samuel 2:22; 4:15,18). Although it was customary for the priest to stand in the tabernacle and minister to the Lord, Eli was so heavy and out of shape that he had to sit in order to perform his duties. Furthermore, he had two sons named Hophni and Phinehas who were exceedingly wicked in God's sight. (We'll learn more about them in a few moments.)

Needless to say, the spiritual environment in Shiloh was quite a mess. Nevertheless, the Bible says:

> …[Hannah] was in bitterness of soul, and prayed unto the Lord, and wept sore. And she vowed a vow, and said, O Lord of hosts, if thou wilt indeed look on the affliction of thine handmaid, and remember me, and not forget thine handmaid, but wilt give unto thine handmaid a man child, then I will give him unto the Lord all the days of his life, and there shall no razor come upon his head.
> — 1 Samuel 1:10,11

Notice the words "vowed a vow." This phrase in the Septuagint, which is the Greek version of the Old Testament, is a translation of the Greek word *proseuchomai*. Out of all the words for "prayer" in the Bible, the word *proseuchomai* is the most commonly used, appearing approximately 127 times in the New Testament alone.

Proseuchomai is a compound of the words *pros* and *euchomai*. The word *pros* means *toward* and implies *closeness*; the word *euchomai* is derived from the word *euche*, which is an old Greek word that describes a *wish, desire, prayer*, or *vow*. When these two words are compounded to form *proseuchomai*, it means *to come near to offer a request*. Thus, this form of prayer — the prayer of consecration — pictures a person who wants something so desperately, they come very close to God and make a vow to give Him something in exchange for a favorable answer to prayer. That's what Hannah did. She said, "Lord, if You will give me a son, I will give him back to You to serve You all the days of his life."

Hannah Honored Eli as High Priest and Received an Answer to Her Prayer

It's interesting to note that while Hannah was pouring out her heart to God, Eli noticed her and totally misinterpreted what she was doing. The Bible says, "And it came to pass, as she continued praying before the Lord, that Eli marked her mouth. Now Hannah, she spake in her heart; only her lips moved, but her voice was not heard: therefore Eli thought she had been drunken. And Eli said unto her, How long wilt thou be drunken? put away thy wine from thee" (1 Samuel 1:12-14).

Because Eli's love for God had grown cold, he couldn't spiritually discern that Hannah was not drunk but in a desperate state of intercession. Amazingly, in spite of his harsh and false accusation, Hannah honored Eli's position as high priest and responded by saying, "…No, my lord, I am a woman of a sorrowful spirit: I have drunk neither wine nor strong drink, but have poured out my soul before the Lord. Count not thine handmaid for a daughter of Belial: for out of the abundance of my complaint and grief have I spoken hitherto" (1 Samuel 1:15,16).

Coming to his senses, the Bible says, "Then Eli answered and said, Go in peace: and the God of Israel grant thee thy petition that thou hast asked of him. And she said, Let thine handmaid find grace in thy sight. So the woman went her way, and did eat, and her countenance was no more sad. And they rose up in the morning early, and worshipped before the Lord, and returned, and came to their house to Ramah: and Elkanah knew Hannah his wife; and the Lord remembered her. Wherefore it came to pass, when the time was come about after Hannah had conceived, that she bare a son, and called his name Samuel, saying, Because I have asked him of the Lord" (1 Samuel 1:17-20).

Hannah Made Good on Her Promise

When it came time to return to Shiloh to worship the Lord, the Bible says, "And the man Elkanah, and all his house, went up to offer unto the Lord the yearly sacrifice, and his vow. But Hannah went not up; for she said unto her husband, I will not go up until the child be weaned, and then I will bring him, that he may appear before the Lord, and there abide for ever. And Elkanah her husband said unto her, Do what seemeth thee good; tarry until thou have weaned him; only the Lord establish his word. So the woman abode, and gave her son suck until she weaned him" (1 Samuel 1:21-23). Hannah knew that the next time she went up to Shiloh, she would need to honor her vow to God and leave Samuel in Eli's care. Therefore, she focused all of her attention on the limited remaining moments she would have with her son.

It is important to note that in those days, a child was weaned — or completely finished being nursed — somewhere between the ages of four and six. This is significant because it tells us about how old Samuel was when Hannah left him in the complete custody of Eli the priest. First Samuel 1:24 says, "And when she had weaned him, she took him up with her, with three bullocks, and one ephah of flour, and a bottle of wine, and brought him unto the house of the Lord in Shiloh: and the child was young."

Normally, the offering brought to the Lord was one bullock (or bull). But in great appreciation to God's answer to prayer, Hannah brought three bullocks and offered them to God in sacrifice. This was quite an extravagant offering — it was three times greater than was customary.

The Bible goes on to say, "And they slew a bullock, and brought the child to Eli. And she said, Oh my lord, as thy soul liveth, my lord, I am the woman that stood by thee here, praying unto the Lord. For this child I prayed; and the Lord hath given me my petition which I asked of him: Therefore also I have lent him to the Lord; as long as he liveth he shall be lent to the Lord. And he worshipped the Lord there" (1 Samuel 1:25-28).

Can you imagine what it would have been like to leave your only son in the care of an old, backslidden priest who didn't raise his own sons very well? That's what Hannah did. How was she able to do it? Good question. She wasn't looking to Eli to raise Samuel properly; she was looking to God to personally oversee Samuel's upbringing and make sure that not only were all of his needs met, but also that he was instructed accurately in the ways of the Lord.

The Bible goes on to say, "And Elkanah went to Ramah to his house. And the child did minister unto the Lord before Eli the priest" (1 Samuel 2:11).

Just How Bad Were Eli's Sons?

First Samuel 2:12 tells us, "Now the sons of Eli were sons of Belial; they knew not the Lord." The phrase "sons of Belial" basically means "sons of the devil." As we read further, we see why they were given that name. The Bible explains, "And the priests' custom with the people was, that, when any man offered a sacrifice, the priest's servant came, while the flesh was in seething, with a fleshhook of three teeth in his hand; And he struck it into the pan, or kettle, or caldron, or pot; all that the fleshhook brought up the priest took for himself. So they did in Shiloh unto all the Israelites that came thither" (1 Samuel 2:13,14). The gathering of a portion of meat was a normal part of the priest's salary. But because Eli's sons weren't satisfied with what God had allotted them, they began abusing God's people and stealing what was rightfully His.

Scripture says, "Also before they burnt the fat, the priest's servant came, and said to the man that sacrificed, Give flesh to roast for the priest; for he will not have sodden flesh of thee, but raw. And if any man said unto him, Let them not fail to burn the fat presently, and then take as much as thy soul desireth; then he would answer him, Nay; but thou shalt give it me now: and if not, I will take it by force. Wherefore the sin of the young men was very great before the Lord: for men abhorred the offering of the Lord" (1 Samuel 2:15-17).

God will be patient and put up with many things, but when a man becomes so offensive that he stops people from coming into God's house and worshipping Him through the giving of their offerings, He draws the line.

Where was Samuel when all these things were happening? The Bible says, "...Samuel ministered before the Lord, being a child, girded with a linen ephod. Moreover his mother made him a little coat, and brought it to him from year to year, when she came up with her husband to offer the yearly sacrifice" (1 Samuel 2:18,19). And because Hannah honored her vow to God, Scripture tells us, "...The Lord visited Hannah, so that she conceived, and bare three sons and two daughters..." (1 Samuel 2:21).

The years passed, and the Bible says, "...Eli was very old, and heard all that his sons did unto all Israel; and how they lay with the women that assembled at the door of the tabernacle of the congregation. And he said unto them, Why do ye such things? for I hear of your evil dealings by all this people. Nay, my sons; for it is no good report that I hear: ye make the Lord's people to transgress. If one man sin against another, the judge shall judge him: but if a man sin against the Lord, who shall intreat for him? Notwithstanding they hearkened not unto the voice of their father, because the Lord would slay them" (1 Samuel 2:22-25).

By this point, Eli's voice was hollow and absent of any authority. He had honored his sons Hophni and Phinehas more than he honored God (*see* 1 Samuel 2:29), and the Lord had had His fill of their evil leadership over His people. Hence, He determined in His heart to bring judgment on Eli and his whole house.

Samuel Heard God's Voice and Answered His Call

Meanwhile, Scripture says, "And the child Samuel ministered unto the Lord before Eli. And the word of the Lord was precious in those days; there was no open vision" (1 Samuel 3:1). During the time Eli served as high priest, he also functioned as Israel's judge, which was the highest office in the land (*see* 1 Samuel 4:18). His lukewarm leadership and the wicked actions of his sons, whom he refused to properly correct, caused the fresh, "now" word of the Lord to become extremely rare.

But God had not abandoned His people. He was developing a new leader who would be loyal and obedient to His word. The Bible says, "And it came to pass at that time, when Eli was laid down in his place, and his eyes began to wax dim, that he could not see; And ere the lamp of God went out in the temple of the Lord, where the ark of God was, and Samuel was laid down to sleep; That the Lord called Samuel: and he answered, Here am I. And he ran unto Eli, and said, Here am I; for thou calledst me. And he said, I called not; lie down again. And he went and lay down. And the Lord called yet again, Samuel. And Samuel arose and went to Eli, and said, Here am I; for thou didst call me. And he answered, I called not, my son; lie down again. Now Samuel did not yet know the Lord, neither was the word of the Lord yet revealed unto him" (1 Samuel 3:2-7).

Although we don't know Samuel's exact age at this time, we do know he was still quite young. Up until this point, Eli's voice represented the voice of God in Samuel's life. Everything the young boy received from God came through Eli. But all that was now changing.

The Scripture goes on to say, "And the Lord called Samuel again the third time. And he arose and went to Eli, and said, Here am I; for thou didst call me. And Eli perceived that the Lord had called the child. Therefore Eli said unto Samuel, Go, lie down: and it shall be, if he call thee, that thou shalt say, Speak, Lord; for thy servant heareth. So Samuel went and lay down in his place" (1 Samuel 3:8,9).

Please realize that at this moment, Eli was the seasoned veteran who had been serving in God's house for many decades, and Samuel was the young rookie. If anyone should know what was going on, it should have been Eli. But because his spiritual ears and eyes had grown dull and dim, he had become insensitive and did not recognize that God was speaking to Samuel. Nevertheless, once Eli did finally realize that the Lord Himself was calling Samuel, he taught the boy how to answer God's call.

First Samuel 3:10-14 reveals:

> **…the Lord came, and stood, and called as at other times, Samuel, Samuel. Then Samuel answered, Speak; for thy servant heareth.**
>
> **And the Lord said to Samuel, Behold, I will do a thing in Israel, at which both the ears of every one that heareth it shall tingle.**
>
> **In that day I will perform against Eli all things which I have spoken concerning his house: when I begin, I will also make an end.**
>
> **For I have told him that I will judge his house for ever for the iniquity which he knoweth; because his sons made themselves vile, and he restrained them not.**
>
> **And therefore I have sworn unto the house of Eli, that the iniquity of Eli's house shall not be purged with sacrifice nor offering for ever.**

Without question, this word — which was Samuel's first personal interaction with God — was a heavy word to receive. Yet, God entrusted him with this prophetic revelation without hesitation. It would serve as a confirmation of what God had personally spoken to Eli a short time earlier (*see* 1 Samuel 2:27-36).

The Bible goes on to say, "And Samuel lay until the morning, and opened the doors of the house of the Lord. And Samuel feared to shew Eli the vision. Then Eli called Samuel, and said, Samuel, my son. And he answered, Here am I. And he said, What is the thing that the Lord hath said unto thee? I pray thee hide it not from me: God do so to thee, and more also, if thou hide any thing from me of all the things that he said unto thee. And Samuel told him every whit, and hid nothing from him. And he said, It is the Lord: let him do what seemeth him good" (1 Samuel 3:15-18).

Sure enough, what God forecasted for Eli and his family became a reality. You can read the fulfillment of this prophetic word in First Samuel 4. When the Israelites went out to fight the Philistines, they were soundly defeated. More than 30,000 soldiers died, and the Ark of the Covenant was seized by the Philistines. Eli's sons, Hophni and Phinehas were killed, and when the news of their death reached their father, he fell off his chair, broke his neck and died. All these events took place in the same day, just as the Lord foretold.

What about Samuel? The Bible says, "And Samuel grew, and the Lord was with him, and did let none of his words fall to the ground. And all Israel from Dan even to Beersheba knew that Samuel was established to be a prophet of the Lord. And the Lord appeared again in Shiloh: for the Lord revealed himself to Samuel in Shiloh by the word of the Lord" (1 Samuel 3:19-21).

STUDY QUESTIONS

Study to shew thyself approved unto God, a workman that needeth not to be ashamed, rightly dividing the word of truth.
— 2 Timothy 2:15

1. What new insights did you learn about Hannah and her family and the birth of her son Samuel? How about Eli and his sons Hophni and Phinehas? Think about each person's character and their relationship with God.
2. The Bible says God was very upset with Eli because he honored his sons more than he honored God. In your own words, describe what Eli did that hurt God so deeply (*see* 1 Samuel 2:12-17,22-25,29; 3:13,14). If you were Eli and you found out your sons were using their

position of authority to abuse others, what do you think would be the right thing to do?

3. Imagine you're Hannah and it's time to honor your vow to God and leave your young impressionable child in the care of Eli — the old, backslidden priest who didn't raise his sons very well. How difficult would it be to follow through on your commitment? What would help strengthen your trust in God to personally oversee the upbringing of your child? (*Consider* Second Timothy 1:12; Second Thessalonians 3:3; Jude 24; Psalms 31:23; 37:28; Proverbs 2:8.)

PRACTICAL APPLICATION

> But be ye doers of the word, and not hearers only, deceiving your own selves.
> —James 1:22

1. It seems Peninnah's relentless aggravation was a powerful motivation that pushed Hannah to the brink of total surrender and moved her to make her vow to God — to give her son back to the Lord after he was born. What (or who) in your life seems to be a source of relentless aggravation? How might God be using it to bring you to a place of total surrender before Him?

2. Like Hannah, have you ever prayed a prayer of consecration — a *proseuchomai*? Have you ever wanted something so desperately that you came close to God and made a vow to give Him something in exchange for His favorable answer to prayer? If so, what did you ask God to give you? What did you promise to give Him in return? Did He answer your prayer? Did you fulfill your commitment?

3. Have you ever had another Christian misjudge your actions like Eli misjudged Hannah? If so, how did you react to their spiritual insensitivity? What can you learn from Hannah's example?

4. Samuel heard the voice of God for the first time at a very young age. Can you remember the first time you heard God speak to you? When was it, and what did He say? Can you still hear God speaking and directing your life? What helps you hear His voice more clearly and regularly?

LESSON 4

TOPIC
David — a Man With the Right Inner Makings

SCRIPTURES
1. **2 Chronicles 16:9** — For the eyes of the Lord run to and fro throughout the whole earth, to shew himself strong in the behalf of them whose heart is perfect toward him….
2. **1 Samuel 16:18** — Then answered one of the servants, and said, Behold, I have seen a son of Jesse the Bethlehemite, that is cunning in playing, and a mighty valiant man, and a man of war, and prudent in matters, and a comely person, and the Lord is with him.
3. **1 Samuel 17:32** — And David said to Saul, Let no man's heart fail because of him; thy servant will go and fight with this Philistine.
4. **Job 8:7** — Though thy beginning was small, yet thy latter end should greatly increase.
5. **Psalm 16:11** — …In thy presence is fulness of joy; at thy right hand there are pleasures for evermore.

GREEK WORDS
There are no Greek words in this lesson.

SYNOPSIS
Our anchor verse for this series is Second Chronicles 16:9, which says, "For the eyes of the Lord run to and fro throughout the whole earth, to shew himself strong in the behalf of them whose heart is perfect toward him…." The fact that God is actively searching for individuals to whom He can show Himself strong tells us that this caliber of people is uncommon and not found on every street corner. Yet, when God discovers such a person, He reveals Himself to and through them in extraordinary ways.

King David was such a person. Although he was by no means a perfect man, his heart was perfect toward God. That is, David's driving desire was to honor the Lord in all he did and live a life that was truly pleasing in His sight. He longed to be in God's presence, abiding in His courts and enjoying His close friendship. In his mind, nothing was more important or rewarding.

The emphasis of this lesson:

King David was a man after God's own heart. He pursued excellence, demonstrated courage, was driven by principle, lived responsibly, and operated in self-discipline and self-respect. Yet the most important thing in his life was his relationship with God. And out of the abundance of love that was in his heart, he wrote psalms of praise to the Lord he loved.

When many of us think about David, it is difficult not to recall to mind his ungodly behavior with Bathsheba and what he did to her husband Uriah. Nevertheless, in spite of some glaring flaws in his life, he is still considered a man after God's own heart. One of the reasons God thought so highly of David is found in First Samuel 16:18, which says:

> Then answered one of the servants, and said, Behold, I have seen a son of Jesse the Bethlehemite, that is cunning in playing, and a mighty valiant man, and a man of war, and prudent in matters, and a comely person, and the Lord is with him.

A closer look at this verse reveals six specific qualities David possessed — qualities we would do good to cultivate.

1. David Had EXCELLENCE

The first attribute we see in First Samuel 16:18 is that David was "cunning in playing." Essentially, this means David operated in *excellence*. This is significant knowing the environment from which he came. He grew up in the small village called Bethlehem, which was barely a dot on the map. It had no great concert halls or sophisticated auditoriums where people dressed in formal attire and went to listen to music and poetry. It was just a tiny rural town filled with common people.

David's Bethlehem home was far from the big city, and his family was usually busy with the daily issues of village life. It is very doubtful that anyone in that little town ever dreamed of becoming a king. It's more likely they were busy dreaming about purchasing a new cow!

If David ever dreamed of becoming king, there is no record of it in Scripture. Likewise, there is no mention in the Bible of David dreaming of playing his instrument before adoring crowds of listeners or worshiping in God's temple with thousands of singers and musicians. Moreover, the Bible doesn't say anything about him lying in green pastures dreaming about scores of future generations singing the psalms he wrote. If David had dreams of this nature, we don't know it from God's Word.

However, there's something about David during his younger years we do know: He was *cunning in playing* (1 Samuel 16:18). Therefore, he had a strong desire to play his instrument like a real professional. He didn't play it for fanfare or applause, and he wasn't looking to perform in some great concert hall. He played his music well and with excellence for himself — just because he wanted to do it.

While he tended his father's sheep, he reached for his instrument and sang to the stars. Hour after hour after hour, he played each song again and again until he could play it perfectly. He also wrote lyrics and expressions from deep within his spirit and soul.

Few shepherds in David's day knew how to write because shepherds didn't need writing skills. But David possessed such an unquenchable urge to be excellent, he learned to express on paper the deepest thoughts of his heart. Again, this was a very remarkable quality to find in a boy who grew up in a very unremarkable setting!

Without question, David had desire, and desire is a person's insatiable urge, longing, appetite, craving, and yearning to stretch for something greater than he is right now. This issue of desire is so critical to advancement in life that when the apostle Paul gave Timothy his list of character requirements for Christian leaders, the first thing he listed was desire (*see* 1 Timothy 3:1). That's what David had, and it set him apart from all the others.

2. David Had COURAGE

The second quality David had according to First Samuel 16:18 is that he was "a mighty valiant man," which means David was a man of great *courage*. Indeed, it takes inward courage to do God's will.

Most often God's orders don't come at a convenient moment or during an easy time in our lives. Therefore, to take on the assignment He gives, we must learn how to deal with voices of opposition — including the voice of the devil, our friends, and even our family. Directly or indirectly, they will often tell us to back up, slow down, or reconsider our plan of action.

Courage is having the guts to do what needs to be done, regardless of the fear you may feel or the questions that remain unanswered. When you walk in courage, you have the endurance, firmness, and fortitude to take a stand and do what is right, no matter what opposition you encounter. In short, courage is having the nerve to do what you know God has called you to do.

David had courage. It was bold and courageous for David to go out into the wilderness at his young age and shepherd an entire flock of sheep by himself for days on end. The very fact that he was given this kind of responsibility at such an early age tells us he was a bold, courageous young man. How many boys in today's world could handle this kind of responsibility?

David did what full-grown men would be tempted to run away from. He stood courageously and fought a lion and a bear to protect his sheep. He took his responsibility to protect his sheep deep into his heart and soul. He was committed to do his job regardless of the risk or opposition he encountered. Without question, David demonstrated courage.

3. David Had PRINCIPLE

The third characteristic of David we see in First Samuel 16:18 is that he was "a man of war," which means he was a man of *principle*. David was governed by what he believed to be right and wrong. He stood up to fight for what was right because he had principle!

Consider his actions when he went out to see how his brothers and the army of Israel were doing in their battle against the Philistines. First Samuel 17:16 says that Goliath of Gath came out every morning and evening for 40 days taunting and challenging the army of Israel. Sadly, the well-trained, well-armed men of Israel trembled at the boldness of this Philistine monster. Even King Saul shuddered in fear when he heard Goliath's threats (*see* 1 Samuel 17:11).

When David showed up and heard the giant's blasphemies against God and his threats toward God's people, he was infuriated and could not keep silent. It wasn't long before David's words were reported to King Saul, and

Saul called for David to be brought before him. David told the king, "...Let no man's heart fail because of him; thy servant will go and fight with this Philistine" (1 Samuel 17:32).

Although David was younger and less experienced than the other soldiers, his sense of principle would not let him overlook the situation. If no one else would be bold enough to rid the world of this monstrosity, David would do the job. His frame of thinking would not allow him to disregard the assault that was occurring. He was driven by principle.

Principle is a person's inward rule. It is a conviction of what is right and wrong; a moral foundation that determines how one sees and responds to life; a rock-solid belief system so ingrained into one's disposition that he cannot ignore it or deviate from it. Thus, it can be called a person's *guiding principle*. The fact that David had principle set him apart from everyone else.

4. David Was RESPONSIBLE

The fourth attribute we see that David had according to First Samuel 16:18 is that he was "prudent in matters." The word "prudent" refers to *the way a person manages his life*. It pictures someone who is discreet, cautious, careful, sensible, and guarded in his life. The word "matters" refers to *work*, *business*, or *money-related matters*.

Being prudent in business was extremely important, especially when you consider the fact that the business David managed was not his own. Think about it. David's father, Jesse, trusted him to be responsible for his entire flock. In those days, flocks of sheep represented big money. The very fact that David was put in charge of his father's business tells us that Jesse believed David was trustworthy and responsible.

Clearly, he had his head on straight in regard to the serious issues of work, business, and money-related matters. While other boys were playing with kids their own age, David was developing and improving himself. Because he was faithful in small things, he was eventually placed in charge of bigger things (*see* Job 8:7). David lived a life that was "prudent" in every detail.

5. David Had SELF-RESPECT

What other quality did David exhibit? First Samuel 16:18 says he was "a comely person." The Hebrew word for "comely" refers to *a man's handsome physique*. It is the picture of a well-groomed, well-developed young man. In context, when the Bible says David was "a comely person," it means he was a young man who operated in *self-discipline* and had *self-respect*.

There are many handsome young men whom we wouldn't call "well-groomed" because they have no self-discipline and no self-respect about their personal appearance. It's a pity to see a handsome young man who looks like a bum, walking around in dirty clothes that are too big for him, his shoes untied and his hair disheveled. That was not David. Even though he was often alone tending his father's sheep, he cared about his personal appearance and therefore operated in self-discipline and self-respect.

6. David Was SPIRITUAL

First Samuel 16:18 concludes by informing us that "the Lord is with David." Without question, David had a personal relationship with God. When he was out on those hillsides in the early morning, at noon, and at night, he poured out worship to the Lord from his heart. The songs and psalms he wrote were the expressions of his inner spiritual condition.

David understood that the presence and the anointing of God were inseparably linked, and he longed to live in and experience both. That's why he said, "One thing have I asked of the Lord, that will I seek, inquire for, and [insistently] require: that I may dwell in the house of the Lord [in His presence] all the days of my life…" (Psalm 27:4 *AMPC*). David knew that "…In [God's] presence is fulness of joy; at [His] right hand there are pleasures for evermore" (Psalm 16:11).

The Psalms are not shallow remarks of a carnal musician. The Psalms convey the heartbeat of God. A stranger to God's heart could have never written such moving and meaningful words. Out of the abundance of what was in David's heart, his mouth sang and his hands wrote praise to the Lord he loved so deeply. Clearly, David was a spiritual man, and the Lord was with him.

Friend, God is looking for men and women whose hearts are open to and longing for Him, just like David. No, David wasn't perfect. He made many mistakes in his life, but his heart was perfect toward God. He was a man of understanding and a man of covenant. He understood what it meant to walk in obedience and faith, and he strove to live in that place in spite of his human frailties.

In our next lesson, we'll take a look at another powerful man in Scripture — a man by the name of Daniel who refused to accept the world's limitations.

STUDY QUESTIONS

> Study to shew thyself approved unto God, a workman that needeth
> not to be ashamed, rightly dividing the word of truth.
> — 2 Timothy 2:15

1. The Bible documents a great deal on the life of David. What would you say are some of his greatest strengths and accomplishments? What story — or attribute — from his life is personally most encouraging to you? Why is it so meaningful?
2. Of the six qualities described in First Samuel 16:18 that David was known to operate in, which ones would you say are most visible in your life? Where do you think you need to come up higher?

PRACTICAL APPLICATION

> But be ye doers of the word, and not hearers only,
> deceiving your own selves.
> — James 1:22

1. Without question, David had *desire*, and desire is a person's insatiable urge, longing, appetite, craving, and yearning to stretch for something greater than he is right now. What would you say you have the greatest desire for right now in your life?
2. Because David was faithful in little things, he was eventually placed in charge of bigger things. This is the principle Jesus spoke of in Luke 19:17. Is there a "little" thing God has asked you to do that you would rather not do? If so, what is it? If you haven't stepped out in obedience to do what He's asked, pray for His grace to do so now.
3. Right now in this hour, God needs men and women with a heart like David — who love Him and long to be in relationship with Him and please Him in all things. If you desire a greater hunger and thirst for God, take a moment and pray: *Father, forgive me for filling my life with so many other things. I want to want You more than anything else in this world. Holy Spirit, fill me with a fresh fire of passion for You. Create in me a clean heart that is totally devoted to You. In Jesus' name. Amen!*

LESSON 5

TOPIC
Daniel — a Man Who Refused Limitations

SCRIPTURES
1. **2 Chronicles 16:9** — For the eyes of the Lord run to and fro throughout the whole earth, to shew himself strong in the behalf of them whose heart is perfect toward him....

GREEK WORDS
There are no Greek words in this lesson.

SYNOPSIS
Time and time again, it has been said by Christians far and wide, "I just want to be used by God." In answer to this timeless cry, God reveals in Second Chronicles 16:9 what gets His attention and positions us to be used by Him: "For the eyes of the Lord run to and fro throughout the whole earth, to shew himself strong in the behalf of them whose heart is perfect toward him...."

Although achieving perfection is unattainable, we can cultivate a heart that is fully committed to God. That is what Noah, Abraham, Samuel, and David all developed, and their lives are a testimony of how God will show Himself strong on behalf of such people. Daniel is another individual in Scripture who gave God full access to his life and became a pipeline for God's power to flow into the earth.

The emphasis of this lesson:

From start to finish, Daniel lived a life of excellence. Even though he lived most of his life as a captive in foreign lands and served under heathen kings, Daniel purposed in his heart to honor God, hold tightly to his faith, and keep himself uncontaminated from the world. As a result,

God showed Himself strong on Daniel's behalf, giving him great favor and the divine ability to interpret dreams.

The Backdrop of Daniel's Life

Daniel was born into an upper-class Jewish family about 2,500 years ago during the reign of King Josiah. Just a few years after Josiah's death, Nebuchadnezzar rose to power over the Babylonian Empire and seized control over the land of Palestine. It was the year 605 BC that Nebuchadnezzar attacked Jerusalem on three separate occasions, and after his third attack, he took approximately 3,000 captives to Babylon from among Judah's royal and noble families. Daniel was among this group.

The journey from Jerusalem to Babylon was about 500 miles of rough and rugged terrain. Daniel made this trip as a young teenager, possibly between the ages of 15 and 17. Immediately, he and his fellow Hebrew captives were thrust into a hostile pagan environment, and their lives were irreversibly altered to reflect their new reality in Babylon.

When Daniel and his three young friends — whom we know to be Shadrach, Meshach, and Abednego — arrived at Nebuchadnezzar's court, they encountered enormous challenges. First, they were required to eat foods from the king's table that would make them ceremonially unclean according to their laws. Second, they were commanded to participate in pagan worship that violated their spiritual beliefs and practices. And if that wasn't enough, their Hebrew names were changed to Chaldean names that honored pagan gods, such as the god Marduk. All these alterations were part of Babylon's reeducation program designed to force exiles to embrace and answer to a different identity.

Daniel Held Tightly to His Faith When He Was Pressured to Change

The name "Daniel" means *God is my Judge*. When he arrived in Babylon, his name was changed to *Belteshazzar*, which means *Bel protects my life* (Bel is another name for the god Marduk). In addition to losing his name, Daniel also lost his language, his culture, and his freedom. This forced assimilation was Nebuchadnezzar's way of making all his captives conform to the kingdom of Babylon. The king wanted Daniel and his friends to forget their homeland, forget their traditions, and forget their God.

Similarly, there are pressures on us as believers to forget our Christian heritage and the standards and values of Scripture and conform to the new trends of the world system. Satan, the god of this world, is using things like movies, music, news outlets, the internet, government agencies, and social media to pressure people into abandoning their convictions and their faith in the One True God and His Son, Jesus Christ. But just like Daniel, we must learn to "…hold tightly without wavering to the hope we affirm, for God can be trusted to keep his promise" (Hebrews 10:23 *NLT*).

From the onset of Daniel's arrival in Babylon, the Bible says, "…Daniel purposed in his heart that he would not defile himself…" (Daniel 1:8). Having grown up during the reign of King Josiah, who rediscovered the Holy Scriptures and brought positive reforms throughout the nation, it is likely that Daniel was deeply submerged in God's Word. This along with regular prayer produced a strong inner conviction to do what was right and gave him the boldness to stand for what he believed. God saw Daniel's heart and gave him great favor with many of the king's officials and even King Nebuchadnezzar himself.

Rather Than Being Intimidated, Daniel Operated in Wisdom and Counsel

In the second year of King Nebuchadnezzar's reign, he had a dream that deeply disturbed him. However, he couldn't remember the dream. So he called all his astrologers, magicians, and sorcerers together and demanded that they tell him what he had dreamed and then give its interpretation. When these wise men hesitated and explained to the king how impossible his request was, Nebuchadnezzar became infuriated and decreed that all the wise men of Babylon be killed.

Daniel, who was considered to be one of Nebuchadnezzar's wise men, was unaware of the king's dream or his decree to kill all the wise men. So when Arioch the captain of the guard showed up to execute Daniel and his three friends, the Bible says, "Then Daniel answered with counsel and wisdom to Arioch the captain of the king's guard, which was gone forth to slay the wise men of Babylon" (Daniel 2:14).

Isn't that amazing! Rather than respond in intimidation and fear, Daniel answered with *counsel* and *wisdom*. And his words were so persuasive and received that Arioch allowed Daniel to go in and address the king directly, asking him for time to remind the king of his dream and give its interpretation. The king granted Daniel's request.

This story brings to mind an experience Pastor David Wilkerson talked about many years ago. He shared how when he first came to New York City and began sharing the Gospel with the gang members on the streets, he was not received well. In fact, one particular gang leader got in his face as he was talking about Jesus and said, "If you preach one more word to me, I'm going to chop you in pieces." To that David responded, "If you chop me into pieces, every piece would still love you.'" Rather than answer in fear, Wilkerson answered boldly in wisdom and the love of God. Not long afterward, that gang leader — whose name was Nicky Cruz — gave his life to Jesus, and many other gang members followed in making the same decision.

God Showed Daniel the King's Dream and Its Meaning

After Daniel secured time from King Nebuchadnezzar, he and his three Hebrew friends diligently sought the Lord, asking Him to reveal both the king's dream and its interpretation. The Bible says, "Then Daniel went to his house, and made the thing known to Hananiah, Mishael, and Azariah, his companions: That they would desire mercies of the God of heaven concerning this secret; that Daniel and his fellows should not perish with the rest of the wise men of Babylon" (Daniel 2:17,18).

Exactly how much time Daniel and his friends had been granted by the king to discover the dream and its meaning, the Bible doesn't say. Nevertheless, we know that the pressure was on them as their lives hung in the balance. If they failed to give Nebuchadnezzar what he demanded, they would all be executed.

But God saw Daniel's heart and answered his prayer.

> **During the night the mystery was revealed to Daniel in a vision. Then Daniel praised the God of heaven and said: "Praise be to the name of God for ever and ever; wisdom and power are his."**
> **— Daniel 2:19,20 (*NIV*)**

When Daniel told Arioch he knew the king's dream and its meaning, he was quickly ushered into Nebuchadnezzar's throne room. There he revealed to the king all he was searching for and gave God all the credit for uncovering the mystery. When Daniel was finished unpacking all the details of the dream, the Bible says:

> Then the king Nebuchadnezzar fell upon his face, and worshipped Daniel, and commanded that they should offer an oblation and sweet odours unto him.
>
> The king answered unto Daniel, and said, Of a truth it is, that your God is a God of gods, and a Lord of kings, and a revealer of secrets, seeing thou couldest reveal this secret.
>
> Then the king made Daniel a great man, and gave him many great gifts, and made him ruler over the whole province of Babylon, and chief of the governors over all the wise men of Babylon.
>
> — Daniel 2:46-48

Don't miss the magnitude of this moment. Nebuchadnezzar — the most powerful man in the world at that time — bowed down with his face on the ground and paid homage to Daniel. He then had all sorts of gifts brought to him and burned incense in his honor. Because Daniel humbled himself before God and brought praise to His name, he was elevated by the king to be ruler over the province of Babylon and the chief administrator over all the wise men.

Daniel Operated in a Spirit of Excellence

Daniel lived a long life and served under two Babylonian kings — Nebuchadnezzar and Belshazzar — and two Medo-Persian kings — Darius and Cyrus. In all he did, the Bible says, "…This Daniel was preferred above the presidents and princes, because an excellent spirit was in him…" (Daniel 6:3). Again and again, he demonstrated four distinct qualities that set him apart as a man of God who refused limitations:

1. He purposed in his heart to honor God and not be defiled.
2. Out of his commitment came great boldness.
3. Rather than give into fear and intimidation, he operated in wisdom and counsel.
4. He humbled himself to obey God and seek God, and God exalted him.

Friend, the same God that exalted Daniel is *your* God. The Bible says, "[He] is the same yesterday, today, and forever" (Hebrews 13:8 *NKJV*). Just as His eyes were searching to and fro in the earth and He found Daniel and showed Himself strong on his behalf, His eyes are still searching for individuals through which He can show Himself strong today. If your heart is perfect toward him, He will show Himself strong on your behalf too!

STUDY QUESTIONS

> Study to shew thyself approved unto God, a workman that needeth not to be ashamed, rightly dividing the word of truth.
> — 2 Timothy 2:15

1. Prior to this lesson, what did you know about the prophet Daniel? What new details did you discover about him in this teaching?
2. Are you wondering what Nebuchadnezzar's dream was that God revealed to Daniel? Take a few moments to read Daniel 2:31-46 and identify the details of this legendary prophetic vision and its significance.
3. When King Nebuchadnezzar's guard came to execute Daniel and his friends, he answered them with *counsel* and *wisdom*. According to James 3:13-17, what is the difference between earthly wisdom and godly wisdom from Heaven? Which do you tend to operate in more frequently?

PRACTICAL APPLICATION

> But be ye doers of the word, and not hearers only, deceiving your own selves.
> — James 1:22

1. The purpose behind the changes King Nebuchadnezzar forced on Daniel and his friends was to reprogram them to conform to the customs and patterns of Babylonian life. What kind of pressures can you identify in the world around you that are trying to reshape your identity to conform to the world? Read Romans 12:1 and 2, and in your own words, write out what God tells us to do to counteract these forces.
2. In order to avoid defiling themselves, Daniel and his friends requested that they not be required to eat the rich foods from the king's table, but instead be allowed a diet of fresh vegetables. What were the results of this choice? (*See* Daniel 1:8-20.)

3. How do you think Daniel's decision to guard his *physical* appetite might be applied to our *spiritual* appetite? Is there anything you're feeding on that is polluting your soul and spirit? If so, what is it, and what can you do to eliminate it from your diet?

LESSON 6

TOPIC

Joseph — the Foster Father of Jesus

SCRIPTURES

1. **2 Chronicles 16:9** — For the eyes of the Lord run to and fro throughout the whole earth, to shew himself strong in the behalf of them whose heart is perfect toward him....
2. **Matthew 13:55** — Is not this the carpenter's son? is not his mother called Mary? and his brethren, James, and Joses, and Simon, and Judas?
3. **Luke 16:11** — If therefore ye have not been faithful in the unrighteous mammon, who will commit to your trust the true riches?
4. **Matthew 1:18-20** — Now the birth of Jesus Christ was on this wise: When as his mother Mary was espoused to Joseph, before they came together, she was found with child of the Holy Ghost. Then Joseph her husband, being a just man, and not willing to make her a public example, was minded to put her away privily. But while he thought on these things, behold, the angel of the Lord appeared unto him in a dream, saying, Joseph, thou son of David, fear not to take unto thee Mary thy wife; for that which is conceived in her is of the Holy Ghost.
5. **Matthew 1:24,25** (*NIV*) — When Joseph woke up, he did what the angel of the Lord had commanded him and took Mary home as his wife. But he did not consummate their marriage until she gave birth to a son.
6. **Matthew 2:13,14** — ...The angel of the Lord appeareth to Joseph in a dream, saying, Arise, and take the young child and his mother, and flee into Egypt, and be thou there until I bring thee word; for Herod

will seek the young child to destroy him. When he arose, he took the young child and his mother by night, and departed into Egypt.
7. **Luke 2:41,42** — Now his parents went to Jerusalem every year at the feast of the passover. And when he was twelve years old, they went to Jerusalem after the custom of the feast.

GREEK WORDS

1. "carpenter" — τέκτων (*tekton*): a person that is highly advanced in whatever skill he possessed; one who makes exquisite furniture, jewelry, mosaics, stone work, or even one who is a building supervisor; where we get the word technology

SYNOPSIS

There is one particular thing God can do that no one else can do and that is search out and know what is in a person's heart. In Revelation 2:23 (*ESV*), He said, "…I am he who searches mind and heart, and I will give to each of you according to your works." One of the most important qualities God is looking for is a certain condition of the heart, and it is described in Second Chronicles 16:9: "For the eyes of the Lord run to and fro throughout the whole earth, to shew himself strong in the behalf of them whose heart is perfect toward him…."

So far in our study we have focused our attention on five individuals who lived in Old Testament times whose hearts were perfect toward God — they were open and desirous to do His will. These five powerful men were Noah, Abraham, Samuel, David, and Daniel. There are also several people in the New Testament to whom God showed Himself strong, and one of those people is Joseph — the foster-father of Jesus. The Bible says that Jesus, God's Son, was conceived in Mary's womb by the power of the Holy Spirit coming upon her (*see* Luke 1:35). God needed a man of great maturity whose heart was perfect toward Him to be a godly father to His Son, and that man was Joseph.

The emphasis of this lesson:

God's choice of Joseph to be the foster father of Jesus was not the result of random chance. The Lord had searched to and fro in the earth and saw that Joseph was an honorable man of integrity and mercy. He had proven himself to be trustworthy with his talents, his business, and his

money. Moreover, he was spiritually tuned-in to the voice of God and quick to obey.

The Bible Says Joseph Was a 'Carpenter'

In Matthew 13:55, we learn that Jesus was "the carpenter's son." Many people have heard this verse and mistakenly concluded that Joseph was a poor, low-level worker, but that doesn't line up with historical facts or the context of the Greek in this verse. In Greek, the word for "carpenter" is *tekton*, which is where we get the word *technology*. The word *tekton* describes *a person that is highly advanced in whatever skill he possessed*. It depicts *one who makes exquisite furniture, jewelry, mosaics, stone work*, or even *one who is a building supervisor*. Thus, the word "carpenter" used in Matthew 13:55 is a very limiting, poor translation of the word *tekton*.

As a *tekton* — translated here as "carpenter" — Joseph was advanced in the technical skills he possessed. He was not a simple carpenter that worked with wood. Rather, he was a highly paid professional. Although he lived in Nazareth, it is almost certain he worked as a *tekton* in the nearby city of Sepphoris. This was an up-and-coming metropolis being built by Herod Antipas, one of the sons of Herod the Great. Antipas wanted to erect a town that would become the magnificent "ornament of Galilee." Accordingly, he poured massive amounts of financing and great effort into its development. It soon became the primary banking center of the Middle East. Many affluent and exceedingly wealthy people flocked to this city and took up residence there. It was a lively town on the cutting-edge of culture.

What's interesting is that most of the workers in Sepphoris lived nearby in Nazareth, which was only about four miles away. More than likely, Joseph was one of these people — working as a "carpenter" (*tekton*) in Sepphoris while living in Nazareth. Most scholars believe he was probably a building supervisor or some other highly skilled craftsman with a great deal of authority. It was in this highly affluent town that Joseph most likely met Mary's parents. History reveals that Mary's father was the sacred scroll scholar who maintained the library of scrolls in the synagogue of Sepphoris. Hence, Mary more than likely grew up in Sepphoris.

Joseph Had a Track Record of Faithfulness

At some point, Mary's parents probably saw Joseph working and thought, *Wow, what a remarkable and successful young man! He is faithful, full of integrity, and well-to-do. He is the kind of young man we would like our daughter to marry.* Indeed, Joseph was a promising young man, and they could see he was very good in his profession as a "carpenter" (*tekton*). This truth shatters the false idea that Joseph was nothing more than a poor manual laborer.

Think about it. If God was going to give someone the greatest assignment that had ever been given in the human race — the responsibility of raising the Son of God — would He give it to someone poor and unsuccessful? Or would He entrust the task to a reliable, successful individual that had proven themselves to be trustworthy again and again? The answer is rather obvious.

In Luke 16:11, Jesus said, "If therefore ye have not been faithful in the unrighteous mammon, who will commit to your trust the true riches?" God doesn't just haphazardly throw out assignments. He entrusts great riches and great assignments to people whom He has found to be faithful in past assignments. In this way, God is very predictable. Based on how He works and the principles taught throughout the Scriptures, we know Joseph *had* been faithful in his profession as well as in how he handled money or God would never have chosen him for this amazing assignment.

In the same way that God was watching Joseph, He is also watching *you*. The question is, what has He observed from your actions? Do you stick with projects even when things become difficult? Have you proven yourself to be a person of integrity? Can God trust you with a bigger assignment? For Joseph, the answer to these questions was a resounding *yes*.

Joseph Proved To Be a Merciful Man

Something else we know about Joseph is that he was a *merciful* man. Matthew 1:18 says, "Now the birth of Jesus Christ was on this wise: When as his mother Mary was espoused to Joseph, before they came together, she was found with child of the Holy Ghost." The word "espoused" here describes the Hebrew *betrothal* process. Joseph and Mary had announced their engagement and they were "espoused" to each other. According to

Jewish custom, couples were engaged for one year before coming together physically to consummate their marriage. During that year, preparations for marriage took place, and sexual purity was required.

It was during this year of preparation that Mary would have relocated from Sepphoris to Nazareth. The fact that Joseph remained sexually pure showed him to be a man of integrity. Remaining sexually pure was viewed as a way of showing God that they were serious about having His blessing on their lives. At the end of the designated year, they were to be joined officially and sexually. However, it was during this time of separation and preparation that Mary became supernaturally pregnant with Jesus.

The way in which Joseph handled this unexpected situation revealed what kind of man he was. Matthew 1:19 says, "Then Joseph her husband, being a just man, and not willing to make her a public example, was minded to put her away privily." The words "just man" mean a *righteous man*. Because Mary was pregnant before they had officially married and come together sexually, it could have been damaging to his reputation. But Joseph was "not willing to make her a public example" and had decided to break the engagement privately. In other words, he didn't want Mary to suffer humiliation and public embarrassment. He truly loved her and cared more about her than his own reputation. This revealed how kind and merciful Joseph was.

Given the fact that Joseph was "espoused" to Mary, he had the "legal right" to put her away publicly/divorce her — and he could have even required her to be stoned for becoming pregnant before marriage. However, he decided to take a merciful approach to the situation instead of a legalistic approach. This means Jesus' foster father — though very committed to Scripture and a man of integrity — was not religiously mean and legalistic. He was just the kind of man God desired to raise His Son.

Joseph Heard and Obeyed God's Voice

Another notable aspect of Joseph's character is revealed in Matthew 1:20, which says, "But while he thought on these things, behold, the angel of the Lord appeared unto him in a dream, saying, Joseph, thou son of David, fear not to take unto thee Mary thy wife; for that which is conceived in her is of the Holy Ghost." Amazingly, even in the midst of an extremely difficult situation, Joseph's heart was so spiritually attuned that he could hear God speaking. God needed a foster father for Jesus just like this — one that was spiritually attuned and who would respond to His leading.

Not only was Joseph able to hear God's voice, but he was also *obedient* to God's voice. Matthew 1:24 and 25 (*NIV*) says, "When Joseph woke up, he did what the angel of the Lord had commanded him and took Mary home as his wife. But he did not consummate their marriage until she gave birth to a son...."

Once Joseph heard from the Lord, he didn't argue with Him nor did he hesitate to respond. Instead, he quickly obeyed what he was told to do. This tells us that obeying God was not new in Joseph's life. The first time God asks someone to do something hard, it is usually a struggle to obey. Obviously, Joseph had been previously tested before God chose him for this assignment — and his past obedience qualified him for the task. Over time, he had developed a pattern of obedience. God knew Joseph would obey His directives, which is another reason He knew He would entrust Joseph with the responsibility of helping to raise Jesus.

Joseph's Actions Display Deep Trust in God

After Jesus was born, His life was soon in jeopardy. To protect Him from the looming danger, the Bible says, "…The angel of the Lord appeareth to Joseph in a dream, saying, Arise, and take the young child and his mother, and flee into Egypt, and be thou there until I bring thee word: for Herod will seek the young child to destroy him. When he arose, he took the young child and his mother by night, and departed into Egypt" (Matthew 2:13,14). This act of obedience was extremely significant.

By this time, Joseph had developed a reputation as a highly-skilled technician (*tekton*) — possibly serving as a building supervisor — in the city of Sepphoris. He had a stable job that brought in a sizable salary. But now God was speaking to him through an angel and telling him to leave it all — immediately — and take Jesus and Mary and flee into Egypt.

Egypt was a very different place from what Joseph was accustomed. To leave Israel and go to Egypt was a drastic, life-changing move into a dark, pagan environment. It meant leaving all the comforts and security of what he and Mary had known and starting over from scratch. He had no contacts or a permit to work. As difficult and undesirable as this move seemed to be, Joseph didn't argue with God. Instead, He promptly obeyed.

This revealed that his obedience to God was far more important than his hard-earned status.

Joseph knew he was to obey God regardless of the cost. He trusted that the Lord would be faithful to provide for their needs. It's interesting to note that the holy family's flight to Egypt came just after the wise men from the east found Jesus and presented Him with lavish gifts of gold, frankincense, and myrrh (*see* Matthew 2:11-15). It is very likely that these unexpected, costly presents were instrumental in sustaining the family during this time of upheaval and transition.

Joseph Was a Spiritual Leader for His Family

For parents, consistency is very important. Joseph was well aware of this and it showed. Luke 2:41 and 42 says, "Now his parents went to Jerusalem every year at the feast of the passover. And when he was twelve years old, they went to Jerusalem after the custom of the feast."

Notice it says Joseph took his family *every year* to celebrate the Passover. This reveals that he was very consistent in leading his family spiritually, which is a father's responsibility. Joseph didn't send his kids to church while he stayed home. He led them spiritually, and he did so by example.

Without question, God's selection of Joseph to be Jesus' foster father was not an accident, nor was it the result of a random choice. He had watched Joseph for quite a long time, and He knew all these things about his character. God had seen Joseph was trustworthy with his talents, his business, and his money. He had watched him be merciful instead of judgmental. He knew Joseph was the spiritual leader in his family and was spiritually tuned to the voice of His Spirit. He had a track record of prompt obedience and was willing to sacrifice everything to do what God asked.

Friend, just as God had His eyes on Joseph, He has His eyes on you. He is studying you to see if you are being faithful to what He has already asked you to do. Are you walking in integrity — doing what is right even when no one is around? Are you merciful or legalistic and judgmental? Are you leading your family spiritually and by example? Do you take them to church regularly and go yourself, or do you simply drop them off? Do you show that serving God is a priority or an option? The bottom line: what good things can God say about you? If you are falling short, don't feel condemned. Simply receive God's conviction, repent, and start cooperating with Him today.

In our next lesson, we will turn our attention to the apostle Peter — an emotional man that Jesus called and transformed into a leader of the Church.

STUDY QUESTIONS

> Study to shew thyself approved unto God, a workman that needeth not to be ashamed, rightly dividing the word of truth.
> — 2 Timothy 2:15

1. Before this lesson, what did you know about Joseph, the *foster father* of Jesus? What new insights have you learned about his character and why God chose him to help raise God's Son? What do you now see that you didn't see before?
2. Legally, Joseph could have chosen to publicly expose Mary when she became pregnant during their engagement. Instead, he chose to extend love and mercy. How do you think you would have reacted if you were Joseph? According to First Peter 4:8, and Proverbs 10:12 and 17:9, what does God want us to do in these kinds of situations? What priceless blessing results from obeying this instruction (*see* Matthew 5:7; James 2:13)?
3. Have you been doing the right things for a long time and it seems like no one sees it — not even God? How do Jeremiah 32:19 and Hebrews 4:13 refute this notion? What does Jesus say about our actions in Matthew 6:1-4? What promise is made to us in Galatians 6:9?

PRACTICAL APPLICATION

> But be ye doers of the word, and not hearers only, deceiving your own selves.
> — James 1:22

1. When God spoke to Joseph and directed him, he promptly obeyed. What does your level of obedience reveal about you? Does God know you will do whatever He asks you to do? Or does He know you will drag your heels and argue with what He asks of you? Answering honestly to these questions will reveal whether or not you are ready for God's next assignment.
2. As a parent or grandparent, one of the most valuable things you can do is be a good *spiritual leader* in your home who is consistent. Stop

and think: *How well am I leading my family? Am I leading them in word only or by example?* By observing you, does God know you care spiritually about your family? Are you showing that serving Him is an *option* or *essential* to experiencing the abundant life He has planned?

LESSON 7

TOPIC

Peter — From Fisherman to Apostle

SCRIPTURES

1. **2 Chronicles 16:9** — For the eyes of the Lord run to and fro throughout the whole earth, to shew himself strong in the behalf of them whose heart is perfect toward him....
2. **John 1:36** — And looking upon Jesus as he walked, he saith, Behold the Lamb of God!
3. **John 1:39** — He [Jesus] saith unto them, Come and see....
4. **John 1:42** — And he brought him to Jesus. And when Jesus beheld him, he said, Thou art Simon the son of Jona: thou shalt be called Cephas, which is by interpretation, A stone.
5. **Luke 4:39,40** — And he stood over her, and rebuked the fever; and it left her: and immediately she arose and ministered unto them. Now when the sun was setting, all they that had any sick with divers diseases brought them unto him; and he laid his hands on every one of them, and healed them.
6. **Luke 5:4-8** — ...Launch out into the deep, and let down your nets for a draught. And Simon answering said unto him, Master, we have toiled all the night, and have taken nothing: nevertheless at thy word I will let down the net. And when they had this done, they inclosed a great multitude of fishes: and their net brake. And they beckoned unto their partners, which were in the other ship, that they should come and help them. And they came, and filled both the ships, so that they began to sink. When Simon Peter saw it, he fell down at Jesus' knees, saying, Depart from me; for I am a sinful man, O Lord.

GREEK WORDS

1. "Lord" — κύριος (*kurios*): lord or supreme master

SYNOPSIS

What happens when a man or woman begins going after God with all they've got? When that person turns his or her attention on seeking to know God's ways and do His will, something incredible takes place. The Bible says, "For the eyes of the Lord run to and fro throughout the whole earth, to shew himself strong in the behalf of them whose heart is perfect toward him…" (2 Chronicles 16:9). God shows up and demonstrates His strength in the lives of those whose hearts are committed to Him.

Although none of us start out looking for God and desiring to serve Him on our own, God has a way of making Himself real to each and every one of us in very unique ways as many times as is necessary to get our attention and turn our hearts toward Him. Take the apostle Peter, for example. It took four encounters with Jesus before he willingly fell to his knees and made Christ Lord of his life. This lets us know that sometimes people come to know the Lord *progressively*, one step at a time.

The emphasis of this lesson:

Simon Peter required four separate encounters with Jesus until he made Him Lord of His life. Hearing about Jesus and seeing Him miraculously touch and heal others play a part in helping people make a rock-solid commitment to Christ. God knows just the thing that will bring each person to salvation, and our prayers and acts of obedience help bring this about.

Peter's First Encounter With Jesus
Secondhand Information

The day after Jesus was baptized by John the Baptist, He was walking near the River Jordan, and John the Baptist pointed at Him and exclaimed, "… Behold the Lamb of God!" (John 1:36). Standing near the Baptizer were two of his disciples, and one of them was Andrew, whose brother was Simon — later referred to as Simon Peter or Peter.

Immediately after John's declaration, Andrew and the other unnamed disciple began following Jesus to see where He was staying. The Bible says,

"Then Jesus turned, and saw them following, and saith unto them, What seek ye? They said unto him Rabbi, (which is to say, being interpreted, Master,) where dwellest thou? He saith unto them, Come and see..." (John 1:38,39). Verse 39 goes on to tell us that these two men spent the entire day with Jesus.

Andrew was so impacted by his time with Jesus that he immediately went to tell his brother Simon that they had found the long-awaited Messiah (*see* John 1:41). This was Simon's *first* encounter with Christ — it was secondhand information he heard from his brother Andrew. All he knew of Jesus was what his brother had told him.

This describes the spiritual state of many people in the world. All they know about Jesus is hearsay or secondhand information. They may have heard *about* Jesus from family and friends and know *of* Him, but they have never met Him personally.

Secondhand knowledge is not enough to bring a person into the Kingdom of God. Nevertheless, our responsibility begins with telling others about Jesus. Even if they don't personally meet Jesus at that point, the knowledge we share with them opens the door for their journey to begin.

Peter's Second Encounter With Jesus
Personal Confrontation

Just like Andrew, we have to take the initiative to make sure our friends and family members have more than secondhand knowledge about Jesus. As Andrew did for Simon, so must we do everything we can to bring our friends and family to Jesus — which leads us to Peter's second encounter.

The Bible says, "And he [Andrew] brought him to Jesus. And when Jesus beheld him, he said, Thou art Simon the son of Jona: thou shalt be called Cephas, which is by interpretation, A stone" (John 1:42).

Simon came to the place where he could be introduced to Jesus, and he lingered and listened to Him. We know from Scripture that Jesus and Simon had a conversation — but there is no record that a life-transforming conversion occurred in Simon's life at that time.

What is truly amazing is that during this second encounter, Jesus told Simon that his name would be changed to *Peter* — indicating that he would soon have a change of character. Jesus was basically prophesying

Simon's salvation. But Simon stood there and was totally unfazed and unaffected by what Jesus said. Christ's forecasted change didn't occur at that moment.

This second encounter — Simon's personal confrontation with Jesus — was his introduction to the Savior and His message. He was close to the Kingdom of God but not yet inside the Kingdom of God. Still, Andrew did for Simon what we need to do for our family and friends — he brought his brother to a place where he could hear more about the Savior.

Although the people you know may have already heard the Good News from you, now is the time to take them where they can hear the Gospel presented clearly by others. It may be that you take them to church or ask them to watch a TV program or bring them to a smaller gathering where Christians celebrate and study Jesus.

Taking someone to a place where the gospel message is presented may seem like a small step, but this step may be needed to bring about the change of heart that will make a difference for eternity. You may know people in your circle of family or friends who fit in this category. Ask God to give you an opportunity and the boldness to bring them all the way to repentance and to a true saving knowledge of Jesus Christ.

Peter's Third Encounter With Jesus
A Personal Experience of God's Power

Several days after Simon met Jesus face to face, Jesus went to Simon Peter's house in Capernaum. This would be Simon's third encounter with Christ. The Bible informs us that after Jesus left the city's synagogue, "... [He] entered into Simon's house. And Simon's wife's mother was taken with a great fever; and they besought him for her. And he stood over her, and rebuked the fever; and it left her: and immediately she arose and ministered unto them" (Luke 4:38,39).

Instantly, this woman was healed. The phrase "ministered unto them" most likely means after Jesus healed Simon's mother-in-law, she got up and cooked dinner for them! Keep in mind this miraculous event took place at Simon's house before his very own eyes. He knows what Jesus did was real because his mother-in-law who was sick was now totally healed.

But that wasn't all that happened. That same night, word spread like wildfire through the city that Jesus was spending the night at Simon Peter's house, and people got excited. Luke 4:40 tells us, "Now when the sun was setting, all they that had any sick with divers diseases brought them unto him; and he laid his hands on every one of them, and healed them."

Are you seeing what was happening? A miracle service with standing room only was taking place right in Simon Peter's own home. This was no longer second-hand information, but a personal experience of God's power. Simon had not only witnessed the miraculous healing of his mother-in-law, but he'd also seen multitudes of sick people healed by Jesus' touch that same night.

Yet, despite the fact that God's power was all around Simon, the change he needed at his core had not yet occurred. This situation is similar to people who have attended meetings where God has demonstrated His power right in front of them. They have seen demons cast out of people and individuals irrefutably healed right before their eyes. Some have even experienced answers to prayer and have tasted of God's power — but they've never experienced salvation and been changed at their core.

Sadly, there are many people who have grown up in church where they saw and heard so much about God's love and power, yet they never allowed the truth to sink into their hearts and bring them to a saving knowledge of Jesus. If no real change of character has occurred at a person's core, it's likely he or she has never been born again.

Peter's Fourth Encounter With Jesus
A Life-Transforming Experience

Luke 4:44 tells us that after Jesus miraculously healed Simon Peter's mother-in-law and the multitude of sick people that showed up at Simon's house that evening, He left to travel and preach in the synagogues of Galilee. It isn't known exactly how much time elapsed between this night of miracles and Simon's next experience with Jesus. But what took place is recorded in Luke 5:1-11.

Simon's fourth encounter with Christ took place near the Sea of Galilee. Jesus was teaching and a crowd began gathering around the shore. As more and more people showed up, it became harder for them to hear. So Jesus stepped into Simon's boat to use it as a platform and asked him to push away from the shore just a little. This would enable Jesus' voice to be amplified off the surface of the water, allowing the people furthest away to hear Him speaking.

When Simon surrendered his boat to Jesus, he had no idea where it would take him. But after preaching to the multitude, Jesus told him, "…Launch out into the deep, and let down your nets for a draught" (Luke 5:4). Now Simon Peter was a professional fisherman who was a businessman. He and his partners had fished all night with no results. Nevertheless, he chose to obey Jesus, saying, "…At thy word I will let down the net" (Luke 5:5).

What happened next was nothing short of a miracle. The Bible says, "And when they had this done, they enclosed a great multitude of fishes: and their net brake" (Luke 5:6). The catch was so enormous that Peter "…beckoned unto their partners, which were in the other ship, that they should come and help them. And they came, and filled both the ships, so that they began to sink" (Luke 5:7).

The haul of fish they caught was so huge it couldn't be attributed to coincidence. Peter had been fishing all his life, but he had never seen anything like this — and neither had anyone else. This fourth encounter with Christ pushed Simon into a rock-solid faith in which he totally committed his life to the cause of Christ.

The Bible says, "…He fell down at Jesus' knees, saying, Depart from me; for I am a sinful man, O Lord" (Luke 5:8). In the original Greek, it says Peter literally collapsed in front of Jesus. In that divine moment, he recognized his sinfulness and called Jesus "Lord," which in Greek is the word *kurios*, meaning *lord* or *supreme master*. Peter finally recognized Jesus as having supreme spiritual authority and surrendered his life to Him.

Stop and think about this life-transforming experience. This happened:

- *After* Simon Peter had learned that Jesus was the Messiah.
- *After* Jesus had had a personal conversation with Peter and spent time in his home.
- *After* Peter had seen Jesus miraculously heal his mother-in-law.
- *After* he had witnessed Jesus healing multitudes at his own home.

One might think that these previous encounters would have been enough to bring Peter to the point of conversion. However, it took this final experience to cause him to drop to his knees and *fully acknowledge* the Lordship of Jesus Christ. This demonstrates how different things touch different people. Some will be moved by hearing personal testimony about Jesus, and others will be moved by seeing signs and wonders. But for Peter, it took Jesus touching and miraculously blessing his wallet. The huge catch of fish meant big money, and that was what Peter needed to fully surrender to Christ and make Him Supreme Lord of his life.

This fourth encounter was so life-altering that Peter never returned to a life of fishing again. From that moment on, he followed Jesus.

Pray for God's Final Touch on Your Unsaved Loved Ones

As you come in contact with many different people, it's likely that you will spend time with individuals like Simon Peter before that fourth encounter that brought him to his knees. So if you share the Gospel with them and they don't commit their lives to Christ, don't get discouraged. If you've prayed with them for God to protect their family or provide for their financial needs and He miraculously came through, but they still don't surrender to Jesus, don't give up. Be at peace. God is still working.

Like Peter, these people may mentally know who Jesus is and may have seen demonstrations of His power, but they have never actually recognized their need to repent of their sins and submit to the Lordship of Christ. They just need *one final touch* to bring them to a rock-solid faith in Christ. That's what you can pray for.

In our next lesson, we will look at the life of a man named Paul — a murderer who became an apostle and turned the world upside down by advancing the cause of Christ.

STUDY QUESTIONS

> **Study to shew thyself approved unto God, a workman that needeth not to be ashamed, rightly dividing the word of truth.**
> **— 2 Timothy 2:15**

1. Did you know it took Peter four separate encounters with Jesus before he humbled himself and surrendered his life to Him? What is this lesson helping you see about the salvation process in each person's life — including the lives of your unsaved loved ones?

2. According to Second Peter 3:9 and First Timothy 2:1-4, what is God's desire for all mankind? What part does He expect us to play? Considering what the enemy is doing to block God's will from happening (*see* 2 Corinthians 4:3,4), what can we specifically pray?

PRACTICAL APPLICATION

> But be ye doers of the word, and not hearers only, deceiving your own selves.
> —James 1:22

1. Every believer has a story to tell about how they came to know Christ and surrender to His lordship — including *you*. So what's *your* story? Did it take you several encounters with Jesus before you gave Him your life? What was it that touched your heart and moved you to accept Christ?
2. Like Peter, the first encounter with Jesus that many people experience is *hearing about Jesus* from one of His followers. Imagine you have 60 seconds to share the truth about Jesus with each and every person you will meet this week. Knowing you have their undivided attention for a solid minute, what might you share with them about how Jesus changed your life? If you don't know what you would say, pray and ask the Holy Spirit to help you put together a reason for the hope that is in you (*see* 1 Peter 3:15).
3. Who are you praying for and believing God to save? Are you the person the Holy Spirit wants to use to reach these loved ones in your life? Ask the Lord to create divine opportunities to show them Jesus through your actions and boldness to speak truth into their lives. You may be the only Jesus they ever see.

LESSON 8

TOPIC

Paul — a Murderer Turned Apostle

SCRIPTURES

1. **2 Chronicles 16:9** — For the eyes of the Lord run to and fro throughout the whole earth, to shew himself strong in the behalf of them whose heart is perfect toward him....
2. **Philippians 3:5,6** — Circumcised the eighth day, of the stock of Israel, of the tribe of Benjamin, an Hebrew of the Hebrews; as touching the law, a Pharisee; Concerning zeal, persecuting the church; touching the righteousness which is in the law, blameless.
3. **Acts 8:3** (*NKJV*) — As for Saul, he made havoc of the church, entering every house, and dragging off men and women, committing them to prison.
4. **1 Timothy 1:12,13** — And I thank Christ Jesus our Lord, who hath enabled me, for that he counted me faithful, putting me into the ministry; who was before a blasphemer, and a persecutor, and injurious: but I obtained mercy, because I did it ignorantly in unbelief.
5. **Acts 9:3-6** — And as he [Saul] journeyed, he came near Damascus: and suddenly there shined round about him a light from heaven: And he fell to the earth, and heard a voice saying unto him, Saul, Saul, why persecutest thou me? And he said, Who art thou, Lord? And the Lord said, I am Jesus whom thou persecutest: it is hard for thee to kick against the pricks. And he trembling and astonished said, Lord, what wilt thou have me to do? And the Lord said unto him, Arise, and go into the city, and it shall be told thee what thou must do.
6. **Acts 26:13,14,16,17** — At midday, O king, I saw in the way a light from heaven, above the brightness of the sun, shining round about me and them which journeyed with me. And when we were all fallen to the earth, I heard a voice speaking unto me, and saying in the Hebrew tongue, Saul, Saul, why persecutest thou me? it is hard for thee to kick against the pricks. ...But rise, and stand upon thy feet: for I have appeared unto thee for this purpose, to make thee a minister and a witness both of these things which thou hast seen, and of those things

in the which I will appear unto thee; delivering thee from the people, and from the Gentiles, unto whom now I send thee.

GREEK WORDS

1. "made havoc of the church" — **λυμαίνομαι** (*lumainomai*): to ravage, to ruin, to destroy, or to devastate; used to describe the fate of people who were mauled to death by extremely dangerous animals; often depicted the devastation left by wild boars, or wild pigs, that were diseased, vicious, and deadly; these diseased animals were known not only to destroy property and livestock, but also to maim, and at times even kill, people
2. "entering every house" — **κατὰ τοὺς οἴκους εἰσπορευόμενος** (*kata tous oikous eisporeuomenos*): going from one house to another house, entering into them
3. "dragging off" — **σύρω** (*suro*): to drag, to pull, to haul off
4. "blasphemer" — **βλάσφημος** (*blasphemos*): to slander; to accuse; to speak against; to speak derogatory words for the purpose of injuring or harming someone's reputation; signifies profane, foul, unclean language; any derogatory speech intended to defame, injure, or harm another's reputation
5. "persecutor" — **διωκτης** (*dioktes*): to hunt, to chase, to persecute, or to pursue; denotes the actions of a hunter who followed after an animal in order to apprehend it, capture it, or kill it
6. "injurious" — **υβριστής** (*hubristes*): pleasure derived from inflicting injury on someone

SYNOPSIS

Our anchor verse for this series is Second Chronicles 16:9, which says, "For the eyes of the Lord run to and fro throughout the whole earth, to shew himself strong in the behalf of them whose heart is perfect toward him…." It is important to note that our perspective of who God will or will not save and use to advance His Kingdom is not always accurate.

For instance, take the man named Saul of Tarsus. Before he surrendered his life to Jesus, he was a vicious enemy of the Church, causing great devastation and destruction in the lives of Christians. Most of us would have looked at him and said, "That is one man who will never get saved." But that is not what God said. When His eyes fell on Saul, He saw who

Saul *would* become and grabbed ahold of his life and began using him to bring the Gospel to the Gentiles. Saul — who became the apostle Paul — is an example of what the amazing grace of God can do in a person's life!

The emphasis of this lesson:

Before coming to Christ, Paul was a madman wreaking havoc on the lives of Christians. Luke likened him to a ferocious wild beast who thought he was doing God a favor by imprisoning and killing believers. Thankfully, that all changed the moment Jesus appeared to him on the road to Damascus. Paul humbled himself, acknowledged Christ as his Lord, and was given the primary purpose for his life — to bring the Gospel to the Gentiles.

Paul Was a Hebrew of Hebrews

Saul was born into a very strict, religious Hebrew environment. In Philippians 3:5, he described the setting in which he was raised, saying that he was, "Circumcised the eighth day, of the stock of Israel, of the tribe of Benjamin, an Hebrew of the Hebrews; as touching the law, a Pharisee."

The first thing Paul said was that he was "circumcised the eighth day." That means he was from a strict Jewish home that followed the Law of Moses explicitly. Secondly, he said he was "of the stock of Israel," which is a prideful statement proclaiming he was a pureblooded Jew. Next, he announced he was "of the tribe of Benjamin." This is significant because the tribe of Benjamin was considered the best of all the tribes.

Adding to all this, Paul said he was a "Hebrew of the Hebrews," meaning that *there was no mixture* in his life. His parents were Hebrew, his home was Hebrew, and his language was Hebrew. He was raised to think as a Hebrew and honor the customs and rituals of the Hebrew religion. Furthermore, Paul stated, "…as touching the law, a Pharisee" (Philippians 3:5). This was his declaration that *he was at the top of his denomination*; no one was more rigidly religious than he was.

Then he said, "Concerning zeal, persecuting the church…" (Philippians 3:6). This was a statement declaring his *religious passion* for Judaism. Finally, Paul concluded by saying, "…Touching the righteousness which is in the law, blameless" (Philippians 3:6). The fact is the Jewish law had hundreds of rules and regulations to follow. When Paul said he was "blameless," it was the equivalent of him saying, "I have kept all the laws as good as anyone could keep them." Although this certainly seems impossible, that was what he claimed. Indeed, in every way, Paul was a Hebrew of Hebrews.

As Saul of Tarsus, 'He Made Havoc of the Church'

As a Pharisee, Saul (Paul) was zealous in his devotion to preserve and spread the religion of Judaism. Thus, he was furious that people were abandoning their Jewish roots and converting to Christ. He saw Christianity as directly opposed to faith in Jehovah and sought to exterminate it personally.

Acts 8:3 (*NKJV*) says, "As for Saul, he made havoc of the church, entering every house, and dragging off men and women, committing them to prison." The phrase "made havoc of the church" in Greek means *to ravage, ruin, destroy, or devastate*. It described *people who were mauled to death by extremely dangerous animals*. Specifically, it depicted *the devastation left by wild boars, or wild pigs, that were diseased, vicious, and deadly*. These diseased animals not only destroyed property and livestock, but also maimed and even killed people.

By using these words — "made havoc" — the Holy Spirit through Luke tells us that before Saul surrendered his life to Jesus, he was consumed with such intense hatred he acted like a wild, diseased animal in his pursuit of Christians. He was like an uncontrollable, diseased beast who viciously attacked and abused believers.

It is also interesting to note that the Scripture says Saul was "entering every house" (*see* Acts 8:3). In Greek, this literally means *going from one house to another house, entering into them*. Saul was making raids throughout the entire city of Jerusalem, looking for anyone who was a part of the new Christian sect. Once he found them, he was "dragging [them] off" to prison. This phrase is a translation of the Greek word *suro*, and it means *to drag, to pull*, or *to haul off against someone's will*. Saul was so deceived that he actually thought he was doing God a favor by capturing and killing believers.

He Was a 'Blasphemer, Persecutor, and Injurious'

No one described Paul's pre-Christ behavior better than Paul himself. In First Timothy 1:12 and 13 he wrote, "And I thank Christ Jesus our Lord, who hath enabled me, for that he counted me faithful, putting me into the ministry; who was before a blasphemer, and a persecutor, and injurious…." This is how Paul described himself before coming to Christ.

First, he said he was a "blasphemer." This word is taken from the Greek word *blasphemos*, and it means *to slander, to accuse, or to speak against*. It indicates *speaking derogatory words for the purpose of injuring or harming someone's reputation*. The word *blasphemos* signifies *profane, foul, unclean language, or any derogatory speech intended to defame, injure, or harm another's reputation*. It is *any type of debasing, derogatory, nasty, shameful, or ugly speech or behavior intended to humiliate someone*.

Get the picture Paul is painting of himself. As a Pharisee, he was dressed in all kinds of religious garb on the outside. But inwardly, he was rotten to the core. He was an *accuser*, which means he was working hand-in-hand with Satan, the accuser of the brethren (*see* Revelation 12:10). He was also a *slanderer*, spewing foul, derogatory profanity and nasty words about believers with the sole purpose of humiliating them and destroying their reputation.

Second, Paul said he was a "persecutor." This is a word derived from the Greek term *dioko* — the old Greek word for *a professional hunter*. The word *dioko* literally means *to hunt, to chase, to persecute, or to pursue*. Just as a hunter strategically follows the smell and the tracks of his prey, Saul was on the hunt, chasing down Christians in order to apprehend, capture, and kill them.

Lastly, Paul said he was "injurious," which is the Greek word *hubristes*, and it describes *one who in pride and insolence deliberately mistreats, wrongs, and hurts another*. His *treatment is calculated to publicly insult and openly humiliate the person who suffers it*. One who is "injurious" is *one who derives pleasure from inflicting pain on someone else*. This helps us understand how Saul was able to stand on the "sidelines" and watch Stephen be stoned to death and enjoy it.

It is difficult for us to imagine, but before Saul was converted, he was, by his own admission, so mean-spirited that he derived pleasure from seeing others suffer physical pain. That's a horrible thing to say about someone, but this is precisely what Paul wrote about his own spiritual condition before he was powerfully converted and brought into God's Kingdom. A careful study of all these words Paul used to describe himself before coming to Christ and their combined meanings serves to underscore why he called himself "the chief of sinners" (*see* 1 Timothy 1:15).

Paul's Radical Transformation on the Road to Damascus

Although that is who Paul was, it all changed in 37 AD, when the grace of God completely transformed him from the inside out. The Bible tells us that after he received legal permission from the chief priests to take his terrorizing ways to other towns, Saul of Tarsus began making his way to Damascus to hunt down and destroy believers. But while he was on his way, Jesus appeared to him and turned his life right-side up. Luke records the event in Acts 9:3-6:

> **And as he [Saul] journeyed, he came near Damascus: and suddenly there shined round about him a light from heaven:**
>
> **And he fell to the earth, and heard a voice saying unto him, Saul, Saul, why persecutest thou me?**
>
> **And he said, Who art thou, Lord? And the Lord said, I am Jesus whom thou persecutest: it is hard for thee to kick against the pricks.**
>
> **And he trembling and astonished said, Lord, what wilt thou have me to do? And the Lord said unto him, Arise, and go into the city, and it shall be told thee what thou must do.**

It's interesting to note that Paul recounts his Damascus-Road experience in Acts 26 as he stood before King Agrippa. And in verses 13 he stated:

> **At midday, O king, I saw in the way a light from heaven, above the brightness of the sun, shining round about me and them which journeyed with me.**

This brightness Saul experienced was the *glory* of God. It was so powerful in its brilliance it physically knocked him to the ground (*see* Acts 9:4). In Acts 26:14, Paul went on to say:

> **And when we were all fallen to the earth, I heard a voice speaking unto me, and saying in the Hebrew tongue, Saul, Saul, why persecutest thou me? it is hard for thee to kick against the pricks.**

Only Saul could distinguish Jesus' voice and understand what He was saying. To everyone else, the voice was indistinct and unintelligible. To ensure Jesus had Saul's complete attention, He spoke to Saul in his native Hebrew tongue.

In that moment, the glory of God had pinned Saul to the ground. From that temporarily incapacitated position, he responded, "…Who art thou, Lord? And he said, I am Jesus whom thou persecutest" (Acts 26:15). The fact that Saul called Jesus "Lord" verifies that he was born again on the spot. Romans 10:9 and 13 tells us, "That if thou shalt confess with thy mouth the Lord Jesus, and shalt believe in thine heart that God hath raised him from the dead, thou shalt be saved… For whosoever shall call upon the name of the Lord shall be saved."

Think about it. In a moment, the Church's most zealous persecutor called upon the name of the Lord — and Jesus' power reached out to lay hold of him. Saul's life journey instantaneously changed directions as, in a split second, he was saved, delivered, and changed into a champion of truth. Eventually this transformed man launched the first missionary activity in the history of the Church and wrote letters to various churches and individuals, which were so full of Holy Spirit inspiration and revelation that God's people are still being transformed by these divine truths today!

God's Will for Saul Was Given to Him the Moment He Was Saved

After Saul acknowledged Jesus as the Lord of his life, the Lord gave him these instructions:

> **But rise, and stand upon thy feet: for I have appeared unto thee for this purpose, to make thee a minister and a witness both of these things which thou hast seen, and of those things in the which I will appear unto thee; delivering thee from the people, and from the Gentiles, unto whom now I send thee.**
> **— Acts 26:16,17**

Hearing that God was sending him to the Gentiles must have been shocking beyond belief for Saul. Remember, he was a "Hebrew of the Hebrews" and a Pharisee! As a Hebrew boy, Paul was taught a prayer that all the Hebrew boys were taught, and every morning he would recite it: "God, I thank You that I was born a Jew and not a Gentile." Jews loathed Gentiles. They viewed them as dirty, disgusting, uncircumcised, sexually immoral, and idol-worshiping adulterers. Indeed, all these things were true, and Gentiles were far from the covenant promises of God.

Jews hated Gentiles with such a passion that they were taught to not even sit at the same table and share a meal with them. If a Gentile was sitting at the table, they were to find a different table at which to sit. The only place a Gentile was allowed to fill in the life of a Jew was to be employed as a slave that washed their feet when they came into their house. But now, the moment Saul was saved, he was told that his primary life mission was to minister to the Gentiles.

Friend, if Paul could get saved, anybody can get saved. Although he seemed to be the most unlikely candidate for salvation, God had a unique call on his life. He also has a call on *your* life. You may not have grasped it yet, but that divine plan is lying inside you waiting to explode into your mind so you can lay hold of it and begin to walk it out. It may take time for you to understand and accept His call, but just keep moving forward and things will fall into place.

In our next lesson, we will look at the life of a young man named Timothy who worked closely with Paul and was called into the ministry as a teenager.

STUDY QUESTIONS

> Study to shew thyself approved unto God, a workman that needeth not to be ashamed, rightly dividing the word of truth.
> — 2 Timothy 2:15

1. What new details did you learn about the apostle Paul — both *before* and *after* he surrendered his life to Jesus?
2. When we read Paul's pedigree in Philippians 3:5 and 6, it appears he had just about everything going for him. But what did he say in verses 7-10 about his own background and achievements? What did he now want more than anything else? What does this say to you personally about *your* experiences and achievements — and even your failures?

PRACTICAL APPLICATION

> But be ye doers of the word, and not hearers only,
> deceiving your own selves.
> —James 1:22

1. Paul painted a horrific picture of himself as a *blasphemous, injurious persecutor* before surrendering his life to Jesus. What about you? How would you describe yourself before you repented and gave your life to Christ? If you could show people a picture of yourself *before* and *after* Jesus, what would be some of the most drastic changes they would see that He's made in your life?
2. Take time to think back and remember what happened the day Jesus made Himself real to you and you surrendered your life to Him. Where were you and who were you with? What was the greatest initial change you noticed that God made in you?
3. God's will for Paul was first and foremost to bring the Gospel to the Gentiles. Do you know God's primary purpose and plan for your life? If so, take a moment to write down what you understand it to be.
4. If you don't know God's will for your life, He certainly wants to reveal it to you. Pause and pray: *Lord, please begin to show me Your calling on my life. What have You uniquely created me to do? And how can I better cooperate with You to walk in Your plans?"* Be still and listen. What is the Holy Spirit speaking to you?

LESSON 9

TOPIC

Timothy — a Teen Called to Ministry

SCRIPTURES

1. **Acts 16:1-3** — Then came he to Derbe and Lystra: and, behold, a certain disciple was there, named Timotheus, the son of a certain woman, which was a Jewess, and believed; but his father was a Greek: Which was well reported of by the brethren that were at Lystra and Iconium. Him would Paul have to go forth with him; and took and circumcised

him because of the Jews which were in those quarters: for they knew all that his father was a Greek.
2. **2 Timothy 1:5** — When I call to remembrance the unfeigned faith that is in thee, which dwelt first in thy grandmother Lois, and thy mother Eunice; and I am persuaded that in thee also.
3. **2 Timothy 3:15** — And that from a child thou hast known the holy scriptures, which are able to make thee wise unto salvation through faith which is in Christ Jesus.
4. **Philippians 2:19-22** — But I trust in the Lord Jesus to send Timotheus shortly unto you, that I also may be of good comfort, when I know your state. For I have no man likeminded, who will naturally care for your state. For all seek their own, not the things which are Jesus Christ's. But ye know the proof of him, that, as a son with the father, he hath served with me in the gospel.

GREEK WORDS

1. "I have" — ἔχω (*echo*): to have, to hold, or to possess
2. "no man" — οὐδένα (*oudena*): emphatically, absolutely no one, not even one
3. "likeminded" — ἰσόψυχος (*isopsuchos*): compound of ἴσος (*isos*) and ψυχή (*psuche*); the word ἴσος (*isos*) denotes something equal or identical; the word ψυχή (*psyche*) is the word "soul" and it is where we derive the word "psychology"; compounded, it means equal or identical in soul; equal or identical in affection, emotion, and in every aspect of the feelings and convictions of one's soul
4. "naturally (care)" — γνησίως (*gnesois*): genuinely; truly; authentically; denotes the feelings a mother has for a newborn baby
5. "for your state" — τὰ περὶ ὑμῶν (*ta peri humon*): the things surrounding you
6. "seek" — ζητέω (*zeteo*): to seek, to search, or to look very intensively
7. "their own" — τὰ ἑαυτῶν (*ta heauton*): the things of themselves; the things about themselves; they are self-focused
8. "know" — γινώσκω (*ginosko*): to have a full comprehension about the person or thing being acknowledged
9. "proof" — δοκιμάζω (*dokimadzo*): a test to determine the quality or sincerity of a thing; the object scrutinized has passed the test, so it can now be viewed as genuine and sincere; used to illustrate the tests that

were used to determine real and counterfeit coinage; to approve and deem fit after appropriate testing; also used to describe the process of testing an individual's character to see if he was deemed "fit" for public office

10. "that as a son with the father" — ὅτι ὡς πατρὶ τέκνον (*hoti hos patri teknon*): depicts a father-son relationship

11. "served" — δοῦλος (*doulos*): tense means "has served"; the most abject term for a slave in the New Testament; pictures one whose will is completely swallowed up in the will of another

SYNOPSIS

In our last lesson, we learned about the apostle Paul, a powerful man that the Holy Spirit flowed through mightily to advance God's Kingdom in the earth. We know from his own lips that before coming to Christ, he was a blasphemous persecutor of Christians that wreaked havoc on the Church. But when the Holy Spirit grabbed hold of Paul's life, everything changed!

In Philippians 3:12, Paul declared, "…I am apprehended of Christ Jesus." The word "apprehended" is the Greek word *katalambano*, which is a compound of two words — *kata* and *lambano*. The word *kata* carries the idea of *a downward movement*, and the word *lambano*, means *to grab or to take*. When the two words are joined to form *katalambano*, it means *to seize, to grab hold of, to pull down, to tackle, to conquer, to master, or to hold under one's power*.

When Paul said, "I was apprehended of Jesus Christ," he was actually saying, "When I got saved, Jesus seized me, conquered me, tackled me and took me down. He mastered me and made me His own." In that moment, when Saul called on the name of the Lord, Jesus seized him and saved him. Saul became the apostle Paul, and through Paul's life countless other lives were *apprehended* by Jesus — including the life of a young man named Timothy.

The emphasis of this lesson:

Timothy was saved under Paul's ministry when he was a young man. His grandmother and mother had passed the Christian faith on to him, and his reputation among the leaders at his church was impeccable.

Timothy served Paul as a good son serves his father and was willing to do whatever was needed to be used of God.

Timothy Was Saved at a Young Age

As we have seen in all the previous lessons, the Bible says, "…The eyes of the Lord run to and fro throughout the whole earth, to shew himself strong in the behalf of them whose heart is perfect toward him…" (2 Chronicles 16:9). One day God's eyes fell upon a young man by the name of Timothy. He was living in the town of Derbe, which was less than 100 miles east of Lystra in the province of Asia. Acts 16:1 tells us:

> **Then came he [Paul] to Derbe and Lystra: and, behold, a certain disciple was there, named Timotheus, the son of a certain woman, which was a Jewess, and believed; but his father was a Greek.**

This verse speaks of one of Paul's return visits to Derbe and Lystra. On Paul's first trip, he was stoned to death in Lystra but miraculously raised from the dead when the believers there gathered around him and prayed. With new life breathed back into his lungs, Paul moved on to Derbe and preached the Gospel with signs and wonders.

It is likely that Timothy — as an adolescent or young teenager — was saved during Paul's first mission to the region. Timothy's mom — a native Jew — was also saved at that time. His father, however, was a Greek — meaning he was a non-believing pagan. Thus, Timothy grew up in a home where one parent was saved and the other was not. In this rather strained environment, Timothy managed to latch on to the things of God and became a remarkable disciple.

Faith in Christ Was a Family Affair

Apparently, not only was Timothy's mom a believer, but also his grandmother. In Paul's second letter to Timothy, he wrote, "When I call to remembrance the unfeigned faith that is in thee, which dwelt first in thy grandmother Lois, and thy mother Eunice; and I am persuaded that in thee also" (2 Timothy 1:5). There are a few very important words in this verse that we need to understand.

First, notice Paul said that faith in Christ "dwelt first in thy grandmother Lois." The word "dwelt" here in Greek means *to take up permanent residency*. This lets us know that Timothy's grandmother didn't just have intellectual head knowledge of Jesus. Rather, she had a *living, breathing, thriving* faith that was always with her. And that faith was "unfeigned," which in Greek describes something *unbendable* and *unbreakable* — something *rock-solid*. This unyielding faith was first in Timothy's grandmother, then in Timothy's mother, and now it was in Timothy.

It is also interesting to see that Paul knew the names of Timothy's family members. This meant he had spent some time around Timothy's grandmother Lois and his mother Eunice in order to know them on a first-name basis. Likewise, their faith must have been quite outstanding to make such an impression on him.

Timothy Had Been Taught the 'Scriptures' Since He Was an Infant

In Second Timothy 3:15, the apostle Paul gives us insight into Timothy's upbringing, when he reminds him, "…That from a child thou hast known the holy scriptures, which are able to make thee wise unto salvation through faith which is in Christ Jesus." It is important to note that the word "child" here is the Greek word *brephos*, which describes *an infant that is still breast feeding*. This tells us that from the time Timothy was nursing at his mother's breasts, she was speaking the Old Testament Scriptures into his soul and spirit.

The word "scriptures" in Second Timothy 3:15 is a Greek term that describes *a little jot, a little tittle*, or *a little mark*. The use of this word signifies that when Timothy was a wee infant, his mother Eunice was telling him every minute detail of God's Word down to the dotting of the i's and crossing of the t's.

His Reputation at His Church Was Impeccable

When we turn our attention back to Acts 16, in the second and third verses we learn even more about Timothy. Speaking about Timothy's standing among the church leaders, Paul said, "Which was well reported of by the brethren that were at Lystra and Iconium" (Acts 16:2). The words "well-reported" is a form of the Greek word *maturios*, which describes *a good testimony* and can refer to *a testimony given in a court of law*.

Hence, Timothy had a very good testimony of the believers at Lystra and Iconium. The leaders had scrutinized him under their watchful eye. That is what the phrase "by the brethren" implies. In fact, Timothy's reputation was so good that they could testify in a court of law as to the quality of his character. They were not just guessing he was godly; they had seen the character of Christ actively on display in Timothy's life. He was a very devout disciple.

Timothy Was Willing To Do Whatever Was Needed To Be Used of God

Luke goes on to tell us, "[Timothy] would Paul have to go forth with him; and took and circumcised him because of the Jews which were in those quarters: for they knew all that his father was a Greek" (Acts 16:3). The fact that the Jews in the region personally knew that Timothy's father was Greek means that they also knew Timothy's father didn't have Timothy circumcised at the time of his birth. Therefore, being in an "uncircumcised" condition, the Jews were closed to hearing anything Timothy had to say.

To break through this barrier and help open their hearts to the Gospel, Paul took Timothy — his spiritual son — and had him circumcised. Timothy experienced this procedure sometime between the ages of 16 and 20, right around the time he began traveling and ministering with Paul.

Now it's one thing to be circumcised as a baby boy, but it's quite a different experience to be cut on in this manner in your late teenage years. How many young men do you know who would submit to being circumcised as a young adult? If you think about it, this says a great deal about Timothy's heart and his willingness to submit to God and to Paul's authority. He was willing to do whatever he needed to do to be used by the Lord and serve together in ministry with Paul.

Paul and Timothy Were 'Likeminded'

You may be wondering; *Did Timothy maintain a heart of devotion throughout his years of service?* And the answer is a resounding *yes*. After serving in ministry for many years, Paul wrote about Timothy in his letter to the believers at the church in Philippi and said, "But I trust in the Lord Jesus to send Timotheus shortly unto you, that I also may be of good comfort, when I know your state. For I have no man likeminded, who will naturally care for your state" (Philippians 2:19,20).

When Paul said, "I have," he used the Greek word *echo*, which means *to have, to hold,* or *to possess*. He was literally saying, "I *have* or *hold* in my possession no man as likeminded as Timothy." The words "no man" is a translation of the Greek word *oudena*, which means *emphatically, absolutely no one, not even one*. Paul said, "Not even one other person is as 'likeminded' as Timothy."

This brings us to the word "likeminded," which is a translation of the Greek word *isopsuchos*. It is a compound of *isos*, which denotes *something equal* or *identical*, and the word *psuche*, which is taken from the word *psyche*, the word for *the soul*. It is where we derive the word "psychology." When *isos* and *psuche* are compounded to form *isopsuchos*, it describes one *equal or identical in soul; equal or identical in affection, emotion, and in every aspect of the feelings and convictions of one's soul*.

Of all the people Paul had met and worked with through the years, only Timothy was *identical in every aspect of his feelings and convictions*. It was with such confidence of their shared convictions that Paul told the Philippian believers that Timothy would "naturally (care)" for them. This word "naturally" in Greek is *gnesois*, and it means *genuinely, truly,* or *authentically*. It denotes *the feelings a mother has for a newborn baby*.

Essentially, Paul was telling the believers at Philippi that he and Timothy *genuinely* and *authentically* loved them. Providing care for them was not just an occupation; it was as vital to them as the care a mother provides for her newborn baby. Paul said Timothy would naturally care "for your state." This phrase "for your state" is a translation of the Greek phrase *ta peri humon*, and it describes *the things surrounding you* or *the things concerning you*. In other words, Timothy had his mind on people and not on himself.

Timothy 'Served' Paul Selflessly As a Son Serves His Father

Paul went on to say, "For all seek their own, not the things which are Jesus Christ's" (Philippians 2:21). The word "seek" in this verse is the Greek word *zeteo*, which means *to seek, to search, or to look very intensively*. And the phrase "their own" in Greek is *ta heauton*, and it means *the things of themselves* or *the things about themselves*.

The use of these words tells us that most people are *self-focused*. They are so conscious of their own needs they cannot see the needs of others. To have someone like Timothy who was focused on the needs of others was truly a gift!

In Philippians 2:22, Paul added, "But ye know the proof of him, that, as a son with the father, he hath served with me in the gospel." When Paul said, "But ye know," the word "know" is the Greek word *ginosko*, which means *to have a full comprehension about the person or thing being acknowledged*. The Philippians knew without any doubt that what Paul was saying about Timothy was true because they had "proof of him."

The word "proof" here is a translation of the old Greek word *dokimadzo*, a word that described *a test to determine the quality or sincerity of a thing*. It indicates that the object being scrutinized has passed the test, so it can now be viewed as genuine and sincere. This word *dokimadzo* also illustrated *the tests that were used to determine real and counterfeit coinage*. For example, during Nero's time, he minted coins that looked like they were solid silver but were actually bronze covered with a thin layer of silver. The Roman people used a fiery test on the coins to determine whether they were frauds or the genuine article. If the coins survived the fire, they were deemed authentic.

Moreover, the word *dokimadzo* — translated here as "proof" — can mean *to approve and deem fit after appropriate testing*. It can also be used to describe *the process of testing an individual's character to see if he was deemed "fit" for public office*. Paul used this word *dokimadzo* to say that Timothy had been through many fiery tests and had passed them all. He was still serving faithfully. Thus, he was proven to be authentic, sincere, and qualified to serve in ministry.

Paul unashamedly declared, "…As a son with the father, he hath served with me in the gospel" (Philippians 2:22). The phrase "that as a son with the father" in Greek is *hoti hos patri teknon*, and it depicts *a father-son relationship*. Paul and Timothy served together in ministry like a father-and-son team. In spite of Paul's rough and gruff demeanor at times, Timothy treated Paul with the honor and respect that a son would treat his father.

Together, they "served" in spreading the Gospel. This word "served" is the Greek word *doulos*, which is the most abject term for a *slave* in the New Testament. The tense here means "has served," and it pictures *one whose will is completely swallowed up in the will of another*. Timothy had been completely swallowed up in doing whatever Paul needed him to do. He was willing to serve God to any extent, and he faithfully carried out every assignment given to him by the apostle Paul just as a good son serves his father.

It is interesting to note that many years later, when a person was needed to serve as the senior pastor at the church in Ephesus, the opportunity was given to Timothy. He was chosen for the task because he had proven himself again and again to be faithful in all he did. It was in Ephesus that he finished out his ministry calling, boldly serving the church to the age of 80.

In our final lesson, we will explore the life of the apostle John — the longest living apostle of the original Twelve.

STUDY QUESTIONS

Study to shew thyself approved unto God, a workman that needeth not to be ashamed, rightly dividing the word of truth.
— 2 Timothy 2:15

1. What new facts did you learn about Timothy in this lesson that you were not aware of?
2. Timothy and his mother and grandmother had a living, breathing, unbendable faith in Jesus Christ. According to Romans 10:17 and Colossians 3:16, what are you to do to cultivate and grow stronger in faith? (Also consider Second Timothy 3:15-17). What can you do to increase this faith-building activity in your daily life?
3. One of the best ways to inflict damage on the kingdom of darkness and escape the snares of temptation is purposely care for the needs of others. What is the Holy Spirit showing you in the following verses about serving selflessly?
   - Galatians 6:10 and Hebrews 13:16
   - Psalm 34:14 and 37:3,27; Romans 12:21
   - Matthew 5:16 and 1 Peter 2:12
   - 1 Timothy 6:18,19
   - Matthew 20:25-28

PRACTICAL APPLICATION

> But be ye doers of the word, and not hearers only,
> deceiving your own selves.
> —James 1:22

1. The Bible says that Paul's life was "apprehended" by Jesus, and through Paul, Jesus *apprehended* Timothy and others. Who do you know whose life has been *apprehended* by Jesus because of you? Whose life has been — or is being — impacted and influenced for Jesus through you?
2. Acts 16:2 tells us that Timothy had a good testimony among the leaders in his home church. In fact, it was so impeccable, they would have sworn to it in a court of law. How might the church leaders in your church rate your reputation? Is there anything specific about your character that others have noticed and commented on? If so, what is it?
3. We see that the rock-solid faith Timothy had was first in his mother Eunice, and before that in his grandmother Lois. Who in your family line has helped pass on the Christian faith to you — or helped you grow in your faith through the years? Who are you passing your faith onto and helping to grow in the things of God?

LESSON 10

TOPIC

John — the Last of the First 12 Apostles

SCRIPTURES

1. **2 Chronicles 16:9** — For the eyes of the Lord run to and fro throughout the whole earth, to shew himself strong in the behalf of them whose heart is perfect toward him....
2. **Matthew 4:21,22** — And going on from thence, he saw other two brethren, James the son of Zebedee, and John his brother, in a ship with Zebedee their father, mending their nets; and he called them.

And they immediately left the ship and their father, and followed him.

3. **John 13:23** — Now there was leaning on Jesus' bosom one of his disciples, whom Jesus loved.

4. **Galatians 2:9** — And when James, Cephas, and John, who seemed to be pillars....

5. **John 19:25-27** (*NKJV*) — Now there stood by the cross of Jesus His mother, and His mother's sister, Mary the wife of Clopas, and Mary Magdalene. When Jesus therefore saw His mother, and the disciple whom He loved standing by, He said to His mother, "Woman, behold your son!" Then He said to the disciple, "Behold your mother!" And from that hour that disciple took her to his own home.

6. **Revelation 1:9-11** — I John, who also am your brother, and companion in tribulation, and in the kingdom and patience of Jesus Christ, was in the isle that is called Patmos, for the word of God, and for the testimony of Jesus Christ. I was in the Spirit on the Lord's day, and heard behind me a great voice, as of a trumpet, saying, I am Alpha and Omega, the first and the last: and, What thou seest, write in a book, and send it unto the seven churches which are in Asia; unto Ephesus, and unto Smyrna, and unto Pergamos, and unto Thyatira, and unto Sardis, and unto Philadelphia, and unto Laodicea.

GREEK WORDS
There are no Greek words in this lesson.

SYNOPSIS
Looking one last time at our anchor verse, it says, "For the eyes of the Lord run to and fro throughout the whole earth, to shew himself strong in the behalf of them whose heart is perfect toward him..." (2 Chronicles 16:9). Throughout this series, we have examined the lives of nine powerful men that captured God's eye and through whom He showed Himself strong. They are:

- Noah — a History Maker
- Abraham — Imperfect Father of Faith
- Samuel — a Child Called To Minister
- David — a Man With the Right Inner Makings

- Daniel — a Man Who Refused Limitations
- Joseph — the Foster Father of Jesus
- Peter — From Fisherman to Apostle
- Paul — a Murderer Turned Apostle
- Timothy — a Teen Called to Ministry

In this final lesson, we will focus on the extraordinary life of the apostle John — the last of the first 12 apostles through whom God certainly showed Himself strong.

The emphasis of this lesson:

John — who referred to himself as the disciple whom Jesus loved — was a teenager when Jesus first called him. As Christ was dying on the Cross, He entrusted John with the unique responsibility of caring for Mary, His mother. In his later years, John would pen five New Testament books and fill the leadership role over the churches in Asia after Paul's death.

We first hear mention of John in Matthew's gospel, where he writes, "And going on from thence, he [Jesus] saw other two brethren, James the son of Zebedee, and John his brother, in a ship with Zebedee their father, mending their nets; and he called them. And they immediately left the ship and their father, and followed him" (Matthew 4:21,22).

John and his family lived in a fishing village along the shores of the Sea of Galilee. When Jesus first called him, he was a young boy. Nevertheless, the Bible says he "…immediately left the ship and their father, and followed him" (Matthew 4:22). The word "immediately" means *instantly* or *in that very moment*, and the word "followed" carries the idea of *habitually following someone as a partner*. After joining Jesus' ministry, John traveled extensively with Him about three years.

The Disciple Whom Jesus Loved

One of the most interesting aspects of John's gospel is the way he described himself. Five times throughout his writing, he identified himself as "the one whom Jesus loved" and not by his given name. John was so powerfully impacted by the indescribable love of Jesus that he always referred to himself in that way. The five places where this description occurs are:

1. John 13:23
2. John 19:26
3. John 20:2
4. John 21:7
5. John 21:20

Take John 13:23 for example. Here John said, "Now there was leaning on Jesus' bosom one of his disciples, whom Jesus loved." At the first reading of this verse, it may seem strange to imagine a grown man leaning on the chest of another grown man. However, the truth is John was just a teenager at that time. Yes, Jesus was his Teacher and Lord, but He was also like his elder brother or even a father to him. The fact that John was "leaning on Jesus' bosom" again demonstrates the intense love he felt from — and for — Jesus.

Clearly, John was with Jesus at many significant moments of His ministry. He was present at the resurrection of Jairus' daughter as well as at the Mount of Transfiguration when Jesus was gloriously transformed and He spoke with Moses and Elijah. Likewise, John was present with Jesus in the Garden of Gethsemane when Jesus was betrayed and arrested by the Roman guards and Jewish leaders. Wherever Jesus was John was. He faithfully followed Jesus and became a notable leader in the Early Church.

Even the apostle Paul recognized John's position and spiritual authority. In Galatians 2:9, he called John a "pillar" in the Church right alongside James and Peter.

John's Special Assignment

John's role was uniquely different from the other apostles because Jesus had given John the responsibility to care for Mary His mother. John shares the details of what took place in his gospel, saying, "Now there stood by the cross of Jesus His mother, and His mother's sister, Mary the wife of Clopas, and Mary Magdalene. When Jesus therefore saw His mother, and the disciple whom He loved standing by, He said to His mother, 'Woman, behold your son!' Then He said to the disciple, 'Behold your mother!' and from that hour that disciple took her to his own home" (John 19:25-27 *NKJV*)

Imagine the scene. Jesus was hanging on the cross, bleeding profusely, and struggling to take every breath. As He was bearing all the sins of the human race and absorbing into Himself all the world's sickness and disease, He had the care of His mother on His mind. This lets us know how important it is to do our best to honor our parents.

Early Church history confirms that John cared for Mary to the end of her life. When he and the other apostles were scattered from Jerusalem because of persecution between 37 to 44 AD, John left and began ministering in various parts of Asia and took Mary with him. They probably settled in Ephesus around the year 67 AD — the same year the apostle Paul was beheaded in Rome.

John's Leadership Role After the Death of the Apostle Paul

Once the apostle Paul had been martyred, there was a vacuum of leadership for all the churches in Asia, which was where the work of the Lord was thriving. In that divine moment, the apostle John stepped into the leadership role vacated by Paul, and he began overseeing all the churches in Asia, providing spiritual guidance to all the local pastors and congregations of that region.

For approximately 27 years, John guided the churches from his hilltop home in Ephesus. John's residency in Ephesus was located just above the Temple of Artemis — one of the seven wonders of the ancient world. It was there John lived with a small community of Christians. This is a fact established by many early writers, including Eusebius, the earliest historian of the Church.

In 180 AD, a bishop named Irenaeus of Lyons, France, recorded that John lived in Ephesus and wrote his gospel at his home there. Sources too numerous to name all sufficiently confirm that the apostle John lived and ministered in Ephesus during the latter part of his life.

Why did John live in a small Christian community on a hilltop on the outskirts of Ephesus? Because it placed him just beyond the notice of Roman authorities and gave him greater freedom to provide spiritual oversight to all the churches in Asia. A higher level of toleration and less scrutiny was extended to people living outside the city limits.

From his hilltop above the Temple of Artemis, John and the Christians with him could avoid the constant pagan pressures that existed inside the city of Ephesus. Had John lived within the city limits, it would have placed the lives of all those who visited him in jeopardy every time they came to see him. But living above the Temple of Artemis served as a perfect camouflage to allow pastors to come and receive spiritual guidance and encouragement in a safe environment.

History reveals that an early church was also built on the site of John's tomb. Later, Emperor Justinian built a magnificent church on this same site. It was the second largest church building in all of Asia.

John's Trouble With Emperor Domitian

In 81 AD, Domitian was proclaimed emperor of Rome, and by 93 AD, his madness had reached an all-time high. It was about this time that he declared himself to be lord and god. Although other emperors had been deified *after* their death, Domitian wanted to receive worship while he lived. Soon temples were constructed in his honor and a new order of priesthood was created that was dedicated to facilitating his worship.

In every part of the far-flung empire, people were commanded to drop their heads in deference as they passed Domitian's image, bow their knees before his temples, or burn incense at temple altars to acknowledge his divinity. Those who refused to comply were censored — that is, they were arrested, imprisoned, exiled, or killed.

Ephesus was the epicenter where worship of Domitian began. In the middle of the city there was a place called Domitian Square, and in the center of the square there was a pagan temple. Initially, Emperor Vespasian began building this temple in honor of the Flavian dynasty of which he and Domitian were a part of. When Vespasian died, Titus his son took over the project. After Titus died, Domitian completed the work, but instead of dedicating the temple to the memory of the Flavian family, he turned it into a temple of worship to himself. This became the first Temple of Domitian in the entire Roman Empire. Thus, the cultic worship of Domitian thrived in the city of Ephesus.

It appears that at some point while the apostle John was making his way through Ephesus, he must have walked past a statue of Domitian, and when he didn't bow his head or fall to his knees in worship, someone saw him and reported his defiance. At this point, John was near the age of 90 or 92. When Domitian heard what John had done — and that he was one of the original twelve apostles of Jesus that was still alive — he sent Roman soldiers to John's hilltop home in Ephesus and had him arrested, placed in shackles, and transported to Rome to stand trial before him.

A Miraculous Deliverance From Boiling Oil

It seems that John was taken by ship to the city of Rome and was brought before Domitian to stand trial in the year 93 AD. Domitian ordered John to burn pagan incense to the gods and to Domitian himself in order to save his own life, but John refused.

The early Christian writer Tertullian gives an amazing account of what happened when John refused to bow to imperial pressure. Domitian became furious and ordered John to be thrown into a vat of boiling oil. Normally, when a person was boiled in oil, they were bound and slowly lowered into the oil. First the feet were inserted, then up to the knees, then up to the waist, until finally the individual was totally submerged. A hook was then thrown into the oil to pull out the victim's skeleton.

This is what Domitian had done to the apostle John. After waiting a short time, a flesh hook was thrown into the oil to drag out John's skeleton. But instead of a skeleton being pulled out, John himself was pulled out — fully alive and unharmed! When Domitian saw John emerge unscathed from the boiling oil, he was terrified. Immediately, he gave the order for John to be forever taken away from his presence and exiled to the isle of Patmos.

During the First Century, Patmos had a reputation as being the worst island prison in the Roman Empire. For 29 years, John had served the churches of Asia with no known legal squabbles or arrests. He lived quietly above the Temple of Artemis in the city of Ephesus serving God's people. Suddenly he went from his quiet existence to being boiled in oil and then becoming a prisoner on Patmos. As dreadful as things appeared, God was still at work in John's life.

John Found Another Hilltop Home on Patmos

When John was sent to Patmos, his status was a political prisoner. And as a political prisoner, he was not given clothes, food, water, or medical services. He was solely responsible for his own survival in the harsh conditions of the island. This is why so many prisoners died of starvation, disease, a lack of clean water, or exposure.

By God's grace, John found an abandoned cave about halfway up the slope that led to the top of the island's acropolis — a cave that he and his assistant used as a home the entire time he lived on Patmos. Interestingly, this cave was located directly below the Temple of Artemis on the island.

It was in that cave that Jesus paid a visit to John, and he received the book of Revelation. The cave still exists today with a small chapel built within its stone walls. It is called the Cave of the Revelation. John described some of what took place during his encounter with Christ in Revelation 1:9-11:

> **I John, who also am your brother, and companion in tribulation, and in the kingdom and patience of Jesus Christ, was in the isle that is called Patmos, for the word of God, and for the testimony of Jesus Christ. I was in the Spirit on the Lord's day, and heard behind me a great voice, as of a trumpet, saying, I am Alpha and Omega, the first and the last: and, What thou seest, write in a book, and send it unto the seven churches which are in Asia; unto Ephesus, and unto Smyrna, and unto Pergamos, and unto Thyatira, and unto Sardis, and unto Philadelphia, and unto Laodicea.**

All that John received from Jesus in that cave he wrote down in the book of Revelation. Although most people never thought John would ever make it off the island, he did, and he brought the Revelation of Jesus Christ with him and eventually distributed it to the seven churches just as Jesus had commanded him.

After Domitian's Death, John Was Released and Returned Home

History reveals that Domitian was assassinated in 96 AD, and shortly afterward, everyone who had been wrongfully imprisoned during the evil emperor's rule was granted amnesty — including the apostle John.

Tradition tells us that John took full advantage of the situation on Patmos, performing great miracles and even establishing a church on the island. When he was released from his imprisonment, he boarded a ship to set sail back to Ephesus. The new believers on the island that had been saved under John's ministry loved him dearly and came out to the shore to bid him a final farewell.

The historian Irenaeus wrote that John returned to Ephesus after 18 months on Patmos. Without missing a beat, John returned to his hilltop home just outside of Ephesus. At this point he was about 95 years old. It was at this time that John wrote: the gospel of John, First John, Second John, Third John, and the book of Revelation.

John lived to be more than 100 years old and was used by God until the very end of his life. He serves as a powerful example of how God will show Himself strong on behalf of those whose hearts are fully committed to Him.

STUDY QUESTIONS

> Study to shew thyself approved unto God, a workman that needeth not to be ashamed, rightly dividing the word of truth.
> — 2 Timothy 2:15

1. Prior to this lesson, what did you know about the apostle John? How has this teaching expanded your knowledge of his life and his role in the Early Church? What is the most fascinating fact you learned?
2. One thing that is clear about the apostle John: he had tasted of the real, tangible love of Jesus. As a result, love became a recurring theme throughout his writings. Take a few moments to look up these passages and identify what John is saying about the true, indescribable love of God in our lives:
   - 1 John 4:7-11,19-21
   - 1 John 4:18 (Psalm 118:6,7; Hebrews 13:5,6)
   - 1 John 3:16-18

PRACTICAL APPLICATION

> But be ye doers of the word, and not hearers only, deceiving your own selves.
> — James 1:22

1. When you hear about John's miraculous deliverance from the vat of boiling oil and the fact that he survived his harsh imprisonment on Patmos, what does it say to you about God's involvement in the lives of His people? How does John's life encourage you and give you hope for your own journey?

2. John was so powerfully impacted by the indescribable love of Jesus that he referred to himself as "the disciple whom Jesus loved." Do you know — *really know* — that Jesus loves you? In what specific ways have you personally experienced God's love?

3. Take time to carefully reflect on the apostle Paul's prayer for the believers at Ephesus in Ephesians 3:16-19. Using his words, create a personal prayer for you and your family, asking God to root you deeply in His love and begin revealing His love for you through your everyday experiences.

Notes

Notes

www.ingramcontent.com/pod-product-compliance
Lightning Source LLC
Chambersburg PA
CBHW060407050426
42449CB00009B/1928